THERE IS MORE INSIDE

SRS Productions Inc.
Dover, Delaware 19903

There Is More Inside: Personal Essentials <u>Needed</u> for Living a Power-Packed Life

S. Renee

Photograph by: Luigi Ciuffetelli

For information regarding presentations based on this book contact:
S. Renee at www.srenee.com or call (302)736-5131

Published by: SRS Productions Inc.
P.O. Box 177
Dover, Delaware 19903
(302)736-5131

ISBN: 0-9773292-1-6
1. Self-Help
2. Motivation
3. Self-Development
4. Young Adults
5. Women

Smith, S. Renee 1967
    There Is More Inside: Personal Essentials Needed for Living a Power-Packed Life

Printed in the United States of America

1   2   3   4   5   6   7   8   9   0

To My Parents:
William J. Smith, Sr. & Shirley M. Taylor Smith

Before I ever read a book about personal development or spirituality, I watched your lives. You both taught me something special.

Daddy, you believed in me when I did not know how to believe in myself. Through your love, support, and wisdom you taught me to never give up on myself, my dreams, and to always do my best. You told me to be persistent and that I could overcome any obstacle. You taught me that I needed these personal essentials: a positive attitude, belief in myself, and to be personally accountable for my actions. You made it clear that these were trademarks to personal freedom. You are awesome!

Mommy, I have never seen you try to live life without prayer. Through your love and life, I've experienced unconditional love. You taught me that it is okay to be unique. You said I didn't need a lot of friends to be special, but I needed to be a friend to be special. You taught me these personal essentials: to never think that I am above my creator or any other human being, to love and show compassion toward others, to live a life of integrity, and to speak words of wisdom and truth. You made it clear that these were characteristics that would serve me a lifetime. You are an angel!

Daddy and Mommy, I've put it all together and now I know that *There Is More Inside*. Thank you for the Personal Essentials Needed for Living a Power-Packed Life!

I KNOW THAT...

there is more to you than what meets the eye. There is enough courage, confidence, and talent inside of you to make your dreams come true. I want to help you to discover the personal essentials needed to live a power-packed life!

S. Renee

> *"Courage is when you are willing*
> *to fall, knowing that you have*
> *the power within to get up."*

What's Inside

Acknowledgments 7

Introduction...10

Chapter 1 .... **13**
Human Uniqueness: Preparing for the Fight

Get to Know the Real You 14

Don't Follow the Crowd 22

You Are Unique With a Divine Purpose 24

Chapter 2 .... **29**
Self-Image: You Have the Power

A Positive Self-Image is Trusting Your Opinion of Yourself More Than
You Trust Other People's Opinion About You 30

Words Only Have the Power You Give Them.................................32

Don't Panic When People Say Negative Things About You.............33

Know Your Value..36

Take It Easy, Slow Down, Enjoy the Process 40

Don't Let Rejection Stop You 42

Learn the Lesson and Get on With Life...46

You Are Perfect For Your Purpose..48

A Positive Self-Image Doesn't Mean You're Going to Be Perfect............51

Chapter 3 .... **53**
Decision Making: It's All Up to You

What's Your Guarantee?..54

Get Focused and Stay on Track! 56

The Choice Really is Yours 62

Eliminating Fear-Based Decisions 65
Making Destiny-Directed Decisions 67
You Can Still Have Peace of Mind...71

Chapter 4 .... **77**
Time Management: In the Interest of Time

The First Step to Successful Time Management Is Change......................78
Procrastination: The Number One Time-Wasting Tactic 80

Chapter 5 .... **87**
Attitude: Your Representative

Do You Have the Right Stuff? 88
Change is Good 90
Let Your Positive Attitude Overshadow Adversity...................................95

Chapter 6 .... **101**
New Perspective: Don't Change Who You Are,
Just Change the Way You Think

Your Options Are in Life... 102
You Need a Plan... 102
Why Have a Plan?... 109
Make the Principles Work for You 112

Chapter 7 .... **119**
The Treasure is in Your Heart

ACKNOWLEDGMENTS

I thank God for my talents, my gifts, and my life. He is the source of my strength, joy, and peace. Everything that I am is because I *know* that He exists. God is my more that is inside.

It is impossible to name all the people who have been a part of my personal, professional, and spiritual development and who have taught me that *There Is More Inside*. I deeply appreciate every person that I've come in contact with over the course of my life. Each of you has taught me something about being better. I deeply appreciate our time together, thank you.

• To my parents, who are awesome people. You have given me unconditional love. To my sister, Wanda, who gives of herself with every fiber of her being. Thank you for trusting me with your life. To my brothers, Willie, Joseph, and Mark. Willie, you trusted me with your greatest gift, your children, thank you. Joseph, you made sure that all the guys knew that I was your little sister and that even when you weren't around, you had your eyes on them. Thanks for running them away. To my baby brother Mark, you hold me in such high regard. I hope I never disappoint you.

• To Joan Burris, my aunt, who has supported my outrageous vision from the beginning. It is hard to believe that I've found someone who is as crazy as I am to take God literally. Thank you for all that you've done and for constantly praying for me.

• To my nieces and nephews, Van, Jeff, Renae, Ginni (Tamia), Jakeem, and Julian—each one of you brings me great joy. I've enjoyed being a part of your growth. Through your lives I'm challenged to be better.

• To my godchild, Amir. When I look in your innocent eyes I see how much you trust me with your life. As I watch you grow, you teach me so much about life and living. My greatest desire is to bring as much to your life as you bring to mine. Every principle in this book and more, I want to teach you. To my brother-in-law Thaddeus Barclay, thank you for the calls and your concern.

• To my friend Kirra Cruise-Streat, girl, wasn't college a trip? We have had so much fun over the years. Thank you for accepting me as I am. To Benjamin Blacknall, I value you and our friendship.

• To my friend and editor Sheri Bell-Rehwoldt, I can always depend on an honest response from you. Thank you for reviewing my first drafts and writing to congratulate me on my first book. You even encouraged me to start on my second book. Thank you for believing in me. To Carlos Holmes, when I called to ask you to critique my manuscript you said, "There isn't anything I wouldn't do for you." Since the day I met you as a newspaper reporter, I knew we would be friends for a lifetime. To Dave Tiberi, although we barely knew one another, you told me that my voice needed to be heard, only man of God can see into the invisible world. Thank you for your time, support, and encouragement.

• To Mrs. Greta Fountain, Mrs. Shirley Bryan, and Rev. Charles E. Drummer, Jr., our paths crossed through the African Methodist Episcopal (AME) Church. My experiences in the AME Church groomed me and set the stage for my success. Each of you was a great part of that, thank you. Rev. Nadine Henry, I also met you in the AME Church. Your calls to encourage me came straight from heaven, you are an angel, thank you.

• To Mr. Lacy Myers, every student in America needs a guidance counselor to believe in him or her the way you believed in me. Thank you.

• And to you, the reader, thank you for inviting me into your life. I trust that our paths will cross again.

INTRODUCTION

The purpose of this book is to help you find your voice in this world and to uncover the personal essentials that are within you: self-empowerment, courage, and confidence. I have come in contact with many people who have been hurt by parents, friends, teachers, and circumstances. Instead of living and boldly walking in their glory, they quietly exist in their pain. You are not your pain. You were created with greatness and for greatness. This book will introduce you to that greatness. You have courage. You have talent. You have leadership skills. You have a purpose. Everything that you need is buried beneath your disappointments, hurt, and perceived negative experiences. But you needed those experiences. It is the very issues that trouble us that lead us to our purpose.

Growing up I was shy and timid. I existed in a state of quiet anxiety. I was taunted by my classmates. They teased and threatened me. But as I looked at the lives of my family, I developed the desire for a different life. My father, for example, shared stories of struggle, faith, and courage. A migrant worker with an eighth grade education, he slept on the ground in chicken houses. He was never told he was anyone special. But he made the choice to rise above and thus surpassed the limitations that others placed on him. He didn't see the "limitations"—color, poverty, and the lack of education—he saw opportunity.

My mother, a high school dropout and wife and mother at seventeen, didn't earn her high school diploma until she was thirty-eight. After courageously taking the first step and experiencing success, she gained the confidence to enroll in college. She earned her first bachelor's degree at forty-six and her second at fifty-six. At fifty-seven, she became an ordained minister. Despite her emotional pain growing up, she never had a close relationship with her mother and never met her father. She made the choice to let her faith and hard work increase her power to rise above life's disappointments.

Our family didn't escape our share of challenges. At seventeen years old, my brother got a woman pregnant. My sister got pregnant at sixteen years old. Neither relationship was successful.

The father of my sister's child walked out of her and his son's life before his first birthday. I was fourteen at the time. The pregnancy, the fear, the disappointment, and the struggle had a profound affect on me. I knew at that moment I didn't want to walk down that path and I didn't want to see anyone else wander down that path either. I began to seek answers for life's social issues. Although I was barely in my teens, I wanted to raise people's awareness of teenage pregnancy so I wrote a play. I became so concerned for my peers that I became a peer counselor. The shy, timid person I used to be faded into the background because of the real issues facing my family, friends, and society. I became a leader at school, in my church, and in my community. I knew in my heart that things could be different and better. I looked for options. I read books, listened to tapes, and asked questions.

As a former producer and host of my own public affairs show, *S. Renee & Company* (PAX Network Philadelphia) and *Studio 57* for United Paramount Network (UPN-Philadelphia) I continued to hold a strong stance on addressing community issues such as teenage pregnancy, drug, alcohol, and tobacco abuse, inequality in education, financial independence, health, neighborhood revitalization, violence, and the impact of negative images on our youth. Over the years, the message I kept getting is that each of us must take control over our own life. That's why I wrote this book. I believe this book can help you, regardless of your age or current circumstances. If you're in the midst of a struggle, it will help you to change your direction. If you are uncertain about your direction, it will help to give you focus and clarity.

This book is best used as a personal journal. I believe that if you read the chapters and complete the statements after serious consideration, the book will help you to better see and understand your own courage, develop a stronger relationship with yourself and others, and help you see and begin to develop the necessary life skills for success. And remember, it doesn't matter how difficult life becomes, enjoy the process of growing and learning, it builds character.

Let go of your addiction of being the victim. Free yourself of the emotional merry-go-round. Your creator has labeled you priceless. He will not neglect you. He will not punish you. He loves, respects, and accepts you as you are. A part of Him lives in you. As He created all living things so that they would grow and blossom, you, too, were created to function properly and successfully. He placed natural gifts and talents in you so that you would share them with others. He gives everyone a chance to offer something to the world. You aren't breakable or replaceable without your permission. The choice is yours. This is your moment! Now is the time for you to learn the personal essentials needed to live a power-packed life. And remember, I'm here to walk this journey with you.

Chapter 1

HUMAN UNIQUENESS: PREPARING FOR THE FIGHT

When my purpose and why it was my purpose connected, it was electrifying.
My eyes were opened and I knew the worth of my experiences and pain,
what I had, why I had it, and what I had to offer because of it.
At that moment, everything began to change.

W ho are you? What do you stand for? What is your purpose? What is your plan? What choices will you make in various situations? Discovering who you are is a journey. Life is dynamic and as it changes so do you.

Who I was at thirteen, I wasn't at fifteen. And who I was at fifteen got lost somewhere between eighteen and twenty-four. At thirty-some-thing, defining who I am is harder than ever before. Why? Because I have more experiences to draw from. Good and bad experiences are rapidly shaping me, just as your experiences are shaping you. Yet, internally I'm doing all that I can to hold on to what I want life to be versus what it's trying to force me to be. In a nutshell, when you live in a world full of contradictions, immorality, and uncertainty it's hard to go for what you know is right. I know this because, like you, I've had my share of disappointments, feelings of uncertainty and loneliness, and fear of change. And I'm still not immune from experiencing these emotions again. But I decided a long time ago that I wanted to live life on my terms.

I've learned that this desire is possible, but there is a price to pay. Taking control and being accountable for your life requires discipline, focus, and sacrifice. At times, it means standing alone. My saving grace was a conscious decision to embrace the process, to grow through the process while holding onto my self-worth despite my hurt and disappointments. Bottom line, after realizing that I had to like myself before anyone else would like me, I learned how to fight for the person living inside my skin.

I was willing to fight for her because I got to know her. I liked her. I understood her. I began to see her value. I viewed her as a good person. There wasn't a doubt that she wasn't worth fighting for. Maybe you don't like who you are right now. Let me suggest that you're not looking at what makes you special. It's unfortunate that many people will use every breath they take fighting for a relationship that doesn't mean them any good, but don't give a second thought to the unique person living inside of them. Perhaps because they don't realize that there is such a being within them? Oh, but there is!

There's a person of personality, character, and substance. A person that was born to make an impact. A person destined for greatness. A person that can handle every obstacle, challenge, and perceived defeat. A person who doesn't have to emulate someone else to feel important and be accepted. A person who refuses to get attention through retaliation or by acting out someone else's pain. A person like this lives inside of you!

GET TO KNOW THE REAL YOU

Our primary purpose on this earth is to solve the mystery of our own soul, and to find the rhythm of our own heartbeat so that we can be of good service to others. There are rich resources within us—the blueprint to our life journey, the solution to overcoming our weaknesses, and the light source that enables us to live and understand life on a deeper, more fulfilling level. We spend an insurmountable amount of time dissecting other people's lives. We try to determine if they're right or wrong, moral or immoral. We wonder to ourselves if they're "keepin' it real." We are intrigued with discovering who people really are and assessing what they are really about. But what about you? What makes you tick? What motivates you? What is important to you? What unique talents and abilities do you possess?

I watched an episode of *E! The True Hollywood Story* about the life of Christina Aguilera. As I watched the episode I felt Christina's pain and disappointment. She is an attractive, talented, and likeable young lady whom many young people look up to. I don't believe that she would intentionally lead any young lady to a destructive path of nudity, free sex, or alcohol or drug abuse. But Christina chose to experiment with sex — very publicly. She posed nude, started frequenting strip joints, and sported an edgy adult look and performance. It was clear that this young lady was "acting out" because of some pain in her life. This doesn't mean she is a bad person. Many people go through this stage. Unfortunately, some people never come out. Like Madonna coughing in the background during the '80s and '90s, Christina was doing what she felt it took to get attention and be a "star." But she's not alone.

Britney Spears, for example, had a 55-hour Las Vegas marriage and just eight months later married another guy, Kevin Federline, who already had another woman pregnant when they first met. Britney has since divorced. Her actions indicate that she continues to fight to find that safe place within herself. Christina, on the other hand, appears to have found a safe place to land. We all have a story to tell about our search for inner peace and purpose. Unfortunately, most often, we look in all the wrong places.

Without judgment and much compassion, I know that desperate people make desperate decisions. I believe that most people are doing the best they can based on their knowledge and experiences. When you or I make judgments about people, we do so subjectively. We see only a glimpse of the experiences that have shaped them.

Some of you may only remember Madonna from the 2003 MTV Musical Awards when she and Britany Spears kissed. But I grew up during Madonna's unpredictable, outrageous reign. It seemed Madonna would do anything for shock value. This is called "branding" in the marketing world. Young people all over the world emulated her. They admired her outrageousness and copied her style.

During an interview with Oprah Winfrey in 2003, after she looked within and found some of her real treasures, Madonna admitted to being selfish and self-serving. She confessed that she thought she needed fame, fortune, and public approval. Now, much wiser, Madonna realizes that these aren't the things that make you happy. She admitted to not understanding where she stood on things, nor did she have an understanding of her place in the world. Oprah summed it up well when she said, "When you know better, you do better." This is a perfect example of what I call, "taking on someone else's pain." When you copy someone else's style, values, or personality you don't know what you are taking on. The blind can't lead the blind or they both will fall into the ditch. Can you imagine all the people who thought Madonna had it all together? They desired her success, coveted her perceived confidence, and tried to emulate her daring spirit. But they didn't have a clue that she was as lost as they were. Public approval and financial success are not the fruits of authentic living. They simply mean that you have talent and the ability to market yourself.

Rapper 50 Cent, whose birth name is Curtis Jackson, also understands how to become popular while making money through the power of branding. He has made a name for himself as a rapper with racy lyrics, sexy music videos, and a street-smart upbringing. He now has contracts, however, to appear in ads as an educated, conservative businessman toting *The Wall Street Journal*. The ads, which appear on big-city bus wraps, billboards, and in magazines ranging from *Vibe* to *Town & Country* show us, according to an interview with 50 Cent in *USA Today*, "(That's) 50 Cent at home in those ads. People don't get a chance to see 50 Cent away from the music." So, who or what are his fans following—an image or the real 50 Cent?

Celebrities have the money, relationships and power to change their image at will. You and I, on the other hand, should do our best to get it right the first time. The image of celebrities comes and goes. They transform themselves at will. I'm simply suggesting that we follow our own heart, not the outrageous images that some celebrities deliberately create to get rich off of our insecurities and obsessions.

During sessions with young people I frequently ask them, "Who is the highest paid and most visible celebrity?" Understandably, they most often name rap artists or singers. It surprises many young people that Oprah Winfrey is the highest paid and one of the most recognizable faces in the world. And Oprah isn't appealing to our lowest nature. She is going within and seeking truth. As she grows spiritually, she delights in sharing her experiences with others. She has guided millions of people to a higher spiritual understanding.

In fact, in 2003, VH1 ranked Oprah at the top of the "200 Greatest Pop Culture Icons." Prior to Oprah achieving historical success, she was sexually abused by a relative, experienced rejection, and tried drugs. The difference in Oprah and some other folks is that she isn't transferring her pain to others. She is sharing her lessons so that others will be empowered to have a better life than she did.

Like Oprah, many people have faced and overcome some very tragic situations in their lives. When we look at a person, we see only the surface. There are secrets hidden in his or her heart that we cannot see. Although we characterize him or her as being mean or negative, they are actually heartbroken. That's why when I think about my life's journey, I often find myself thanking God for my life because I know that I couldn't successfully live someone else's.

Thus, I could stop wishing for bigger breasts and a smaller nose. Those were only outward, superficial improvements that would feed my ego. My internal battle brought me to the point of understanding that the time that I was spending on frivolous, unproductive, confidence-stripping thoughts of external beauty, should be spent on getting to know and understand myself. There was only one problem: my ego was in the way. Let me tell you, I had my work cut out for me! I liked it when people told me how great I was—how talented, intelligent, and attractive I was. It gave me an external confidence, but inside I still didn't own this belief within myself. I would sabotage great opportunities and blame others when I "failed." Deep within I doubted my abilities and, like most, questioned my existence.

As I've grown wiser, however, I learned that ego is a barrier to the greatness that is inside of us. And the journey to fix the problem can be turbulent, at times, but the rewards are greater. I say this because when you are able to see your ego for what it is, you'll notice how opposite it is from spirit.

I began my new journey to change by writing down my thoughts and actions that I knew were my ego. To face this part of me was difficult and disappointing at times. I couldn't believe how much of who I was was coming from ego. I soon began to notice how often I talked about myself. How many times I wanted others to hear my point of view that, of course, I thought was right. Do you find yourself always wanting to be right? Do you want people to think that you're someone important?

Our ego can be a very destructive force in our life. It lies to us by creating the illusion that we need to be right. It stresses us out by telling us that we have to impress others. My ego separated me from who I really was. I had to overcome this part of me by becoming sensitive to the sensations of my soul. The information I received from my soul was sent to my spirit. It raised my consciousness and made me accountable for my thoughts, actions, and inconsistencies. I would wake up in the middle of the night and ask myself questions like, "Why did you say that? Why did you do that? What needs to be fixed in how you see yourself, others, and their perception of you? What do you need to connect with internally to fix it?"

The most wonderful thing about this experience was that there wasn't one moment when I felt I was being chastised by God. I never thought that I was some horrible person with a dual personality. I knew that it was my desire to change and to operate more from a conscious level, that would awake me and lead me to truth in the wee hours of the morning. Yes, God was there to open my eyes to what He had placed inside of me, but my conscious decision to find and experience my true, unique spiritual self led me to truth without fear of judgment or chastisement.

This process required me to understand the place where I was currently operating. Once I understood what was driving me to do and say certain things, I had the power to let them go and embrace the spirit person.

In the beginning, my ego tried to frustrate me, as it wanted its control back. However, I understood that the purpose was for God to grant me more of those things that were good for me in every aspect of my life. Do you want to live a more fulfilling life? Then start by letting go of the artificial external stuff that you think makes you who you are. Look within your heart and soul for the truth. In the quiet, invisible space within yourself ask, "Who am I?" You'll find a remarkable, dynamic person.

As I am learning to live on a conscious level, I can see how the process continuously adds tremendous value to my life. Because I ask and receive understanding of why I do what I do. When I see that I'm operating from ego, I simply require more from my soul. Everyone has a soul and ego. Each day we grow and learn from that which we seek the most information. I understand why ego is so popular. Nearly everything that we learn serves our ego. For example, how many different clothing designers can you name? How many inspirational writers can you name? I bet your ability to list clothing designers outweighed your ability to name inspirational writers. We learn very early about how to look good on the outside. But, from experience, I promise you that your most difficult task in life is learning to live from the inside out. The outside is easy to fix. As an image consultant, I teach people how to look and sound important. I can help nearly anyone look, sound, and present themselves as someone practically everyone would want to know. However, in order to maintain that connection with others you have to know that *There Is More Inside.*

I understand that life changes us as we grow up, lose our innocence, and find ways to survive. We see some of the human injustices of this world, we begin to see life as a game. We think that we can outsmart it. That's impossible. The universe was created and continues to operate on spiritual principles. These principles are undeniable and unavoidable. You'll never outwit the system because the system wasn't established by man. Even if it seems that wrong is right and right is wrong, the reality is no man or woman has the power to undo what God has done. I know from experience that some experiences can lead us to a painful state. We learn our parents aren't perfect, so we're disappointed. We innocently enter into a relationship, and later discover that it was one lie after another, so we seek revenge. Friends betray us, so we retaliate. Our eyes are open to the fact that man's system isn't fair so we desert our values. But is this what we really want to do? When we desert who we really are does it make us feel better? Are we really better?

These situations can sometimes cause the inner person to jump up and down in a temper tantrum questioning if there is any loyalty, love, or honesty anywhere. If we're not careful it can devastate and take us off course. These and other disappointments can cause us to stray from who we really are. We'll talk ourselves out of our dreams. We'll begin to think "What's the use?" We'll find ourselves looking at others and justifying our behavior by saying, "But everybody's doing it." The point is, don't define yourself by your circumstances. And don't look at other people's behavior for answers. The truth lies within you. Life and situations in our lives are always changing. As you grow, gain wisdom and look within, you'll find strength and know how to best handle those situations.

There will be times in your life when you feel like you have given your all, and the people and the events in your life fail you. This feels extremely lonely, doesn't it? But despite what you may be feeling, the world isn't against you. And although you may feel like God has abandoned you, He hasn't. Life is offering you one of its greatest gifts, an opportunity to learn more about yourself and about living. These unpleasant events aren't a permission slip to abandon the real you. Instead, they are your greatest opportunity to develop a deeper relationship with yourself. If you learn the lesson, your inner strength and best qualities will come forward. And I promise that when you get to the other side, you'll realize it was power for your journey and a necessity for your destiny.

Life is not an accident. The challenges, victories, and disappointments in our lives are not accidents. They're a part of a divine process that is greater, in most cases, than what we can see or understand at the time. It is God's way of introducing us to ourselves. In life we go through things so that we will let go of our ego and learn to listen and feel the vibration of our soul. In doing so, we develop strength, wisdom, and perseverance that we never knew existed within us. When our circumstances force us to go deep within ourselves, we are introduced to greatness, love, and power.

The process isn't to hurt us, but to teach and develop us. It's all prep work for the next step and the big picture. It helps us to obtain wisdom. It opens our eyes to truth. We can now see clearer and further then ever before. Each time we are forced to find more courage within ourselves, we go deeper and learn more about ourselves. Don't resist change, embrace it. You'll always find that *There Is More Inside*.

I watched a friend evolve through this process. He divorced after seventeen years of marriage. He and his wife have three children. Although he had had affairs and failed to be attentive to his wife over the course of their marriage, it didn't occur to him that his egotistical ways were destroying his family. As he puts it, "I wasn't in a relationship, I was acting out a role." He was devastated to learn that his wife also had an affair. Although he is now divorced, through his suffering, he has learned a lot about the value of relationships, communication, integrity, and the impact of his choices on himself and others. He has also learned the importance of looking inward for personal satisfaction and healing. He now teaches other men how to love themselves and develop a deeper connection with their loved ones.

DON'T FOLLOW THE CROWD

Many people allow this process to move them as it wishes. That's fine if you want to flip through life like a fish out of water, flipping and flopping trying to please everyone, while suffocating yourself. You'll know that you are going in the wrong direction when you find yourself making excuses for doing things that you never thought you would do.

For example, I recently met a freshman at Bowie State University, in Bowie, Maryland. He has a 3.7 grade point average and is majoring in social work. He is confident, attractive, charismatic, and obviously smart. He grew up in a family with traditional values, which expressed great concern with his new fashion sense. He has earrings in both ears, one in his tongue, and tattoos. I wanted to get his perspective on his style so I introduced myself, and after brief conversation I said, "I'm curious to understand why some young people pierce their tongues, tattoo their bodies, and why some men wear big diamond earrings." He said, "Girls don't like good guys." When I asked why he was trying to impress "girls" with body art he said, "Oh, I'm not talking about me. I do it because I'm unique." He even confessed that it was just a college "thing" and that after he graduates he is going to get rid of the jewelry and cover his tattoos. After about a 15-minute conversation, I learned that he felt that what he had to genuinely offer a woman wasn't enough. He was depending on "hip" external things to attract a woman.

According to an article written by Edward L. Kenny that was published in *The News Journal*, a newspaper in Wilmington, Delaware, titled, "Oral Piercing a Costly Idea," Mr. Kenny interviewed Jennifer Redmond, a nineteen-year-old. When asked why she decided to get her tongue pierced, she was quoted as saying, "I just took a risk on it knowing a lot of my friends had this..." I really appreciated Jennifer's honesty, because when I talk to young people most of them tell me that it is a form of self-expression as the young man did. Despite what he said, I think his first response was the truth. If it is self-expression, then why are so many people doing it? I think people do it because "it's hip, it's in, so you do it." Yes, it is expression, but is it self-expression if you are doing it because it's a popular fad?

Dr. John Brooks, a clinical associate professor at the University of Maryland Dental School in Baltimore, claims that "Every year there's more and more stuff coming out." And some of it can cause bodily harm. "We're just better able to now define the extent of injury," says Brooks. For example, oral piercing can chip teeth and rub against gums, even loosening teeth in some cases. Another dentist, with twenty patients with oral jewelry, was quoted in the same article as saying he had to send two patients for gum grafts. "They've literally torn up the gums on the back of their lower front teeth," he said. "I've told them, 'You're going to lose your front teeth because they're wearing so badly.'"

I'm not sharing this information with you to scare you or cramp your style. I do, however, want to raise your awareness of the high cost of sacrificing your own uniqueness for popularity's sake. Be brave, create your own style. Define how you want to be perceived. Take a chance on you. You have everything to gain. If you want to express yourself, then let the uniqueness of that self-expression originate from within you. Otherwise, be honest with yourself. Admit that you're trying to fit in; trying to be what someone else has defined as "hip."

YOU ARE UNIQUE WITH A DIVINE PURPOSE

You are unique and there is a purpose for your life. Once you accept the fact that you are special and that you have a purpose, you'll refuse to treat your life and choices carelessly. The world's greatest golf ball striker, Moe Norman, is a prime example of this concept. Outside of avid golf fans, many people probably don't know who Moe Norman was. He crossed over in 2004.

When Moe was five years old, he was hit by a car. His parents didn't take him to a doctor. I don't know how the accident affected Moe, but he had a speech impediment, which caused him to repeat himself. In addition, he wore mismatched clothes that were stained and he failed to follow the rules of etiquette. By displaying his uniqueness, his classmates picked on him. This made him feel alone. Looking for a place where he could feel complete and significant, at eight years old he found it at the driving range of a golf course.

Moe enjoyed the feeling of freedom and serenity so much that every day he would hit golf balls until his hands were raw and bleeding. Finding his purpose and living his passion paid off. In the '60s and early '70s, he dominated the Canadian Tour. He won the Canadian Senior PGA seven times. While on the international PGA tour, however, he was humiliated by PGA officials and a player who told him to dress better and to quit the shenanigans. He left the tour with little money, but kept his purpose, passion, and personal value intact.

After years of living out of his car, a physicist contacted him. He wanted to understand how Moe could with precise accuracy and consistency strike the golf ball—defying the rules of convention. In the end, Moe conducted clinics at Natural Golf and the president of Titlist committed to paying him $5000.00 a month for the rest of his life.

The three primary reasons some people don't get lost on the wrong path are:

1. They trust those whom they know love them, and are more experienced than them. They don't guess their way through life. They look for and listen to answers that make sense.

2. They understand their internal power and use it. They aren't shaken by people or their perceived mistakes. They stay focused on their purpose.

3. They know that they are different and that is okay. They don't hide their uniqueness, they embrace it and let it work for them.

You don't have to look like everyone else. You don't have to act like everyone else. Once you find that place within yourself, like Moe Norman did, you'll see that the world has already made room for you.

As a teenager, I was concerned about teenage pregnancy. I spoke against the use of drugs and alcohol, even when it wasn't popular. I talked to my classmates about their problems. I felt the pain of my classmates whose parents weren't there for them, or whose life seemed more challenging than mine. I felt like I was in the right place when I was encouraging or inspiring someone. Talking about personal development was like an out-of-body experience. I got high on it. A real, authentic, natural high. It was at those moments that nothing else mattered. I now realize that this desire was what God placed inside of me. God has also placed passion inside of you that leads to your purpose.

I don't want to mislead you. Although I started studying personal development at an early age, I most certainly wasn't born this way. Before I could become that person I had to overcome the first hurdle of learning how to stand within myself. My second greatest challenge has been to understand and answer the question, "Where do my talents fit?" Have you ever asked yourself that question? One day God spoke to my heart and made it clear that everyone has a divine appointment. There are people who need you. They need to feel and experience your personality and style. There are people that no one can touch in just the way that you can. They are assigned to you and you are assigned to them. Regardless of your passion or how many people are doing what you would love to do, if you capture the dream and turn your dream into a vision, you will manifest the movie in your mind.

Does this all sound as confusing and uncertain to you as it did for me when I first received the message? Like a lot of what God says to me, it didn't make much sense at the time. I'm a "prove it to me" kind of person. God, however, acts according to our faith. Therefore, there was conflict. God was saying to me, "I respond to your faith." I was saying, "No, you need to prove to me that if I invest my time into my dream I'll be successful."

Well, because it is God's will for all of us to complete our earthly assignment and He responds to our true needs, one day I was inspired to look at my book and audio tape shelf, which is overflowing with various successful self-help authors. At that moment, I realized that each author and motivational speaker had left an imprint on my life. The impact wasn't the same, however, for every author. I realized that, like them, God had made provisions for my success and your success. At that point, I had two options. I could either accept the truth that my soul was telling me and take action or I could continue to debate the point within myself and do nothing. How about you, what are you going to do?

Take a moment to think about and complete the following statements

1. I am...

_____

_____

_____

2. I stand for...

_____

_____

_____

3. I'm motivated by...

_____

_____

_____

4. I'm most talented at...

_____

_____

5. I'm naturally good at...

_____

_____

6. I enjoy reading about...

_____

_____

7. I enjoy talking about...

_____

_____

8. I can see my uniqueness when I...

_____

_____

9. My unique qualities are...

_____

_____

_____

10. I will celebrate my uniqueness by...

_____

_____

_____

Chapter 2

SELF-IMAGE:
YOU HAVE THE POWER

I knew that it was my fight and only I had the weapons to win.
So, I didn't talk about it.
I just fought with prayer, affirmation,
and the vision that God had already shown me for my life.

Everyone's talking about self-image. I'm referring to what some people have defined as "feeling good about yourself." As a teenager, I was an avid reader of self-help books, but still wondered what feeling good about myself really meant. I needed to understand its meaning in the simplest terms. When do I really feel good about me? What makes me feel good about me? How am I supposed to feel when I feel good about me? And what would I be doing if I felt good about me?

As far as I was concerned, feeling good about me would come and go based on the moment. If the experience was good, I would relish in a pool of pride. When the experience didn't produce the desired outcome, I would, in detail, replay in my mind everything I did wrong. I would question my ability and wonder what the naysayers (haters, as they are called today) were saying about me.

A POSITIVE SELF-IMAGE IS TRUSTING YOUR OPINION OF YOURSELF MORE THAN YOU TRUST OTHER PEOPLE'S OPINION ABOUT YOU

It's that simple. That's why it's so important to know yourself—what you want and what your values are. Knowing yourself empowers you to override all the negative words that have been spoken to you and about you with your own truth of who you are. Let me explain.

Have you ever been called a name other than the name your parents gave you? Or teased about something you were sensitive about? You know, teased about something you noticed about yourself, but thought no one else noticed until that dreadful moment when you were teased about it? Since I can remember, people teased me about the size of my nose, the gap in my teeth, my wrinkled hands, and the challenge I faced when reading in public.

I hated to read aloud in front of a group. It was one of my most horrifying educational experiences. From elementary school through college, reading aloud turned me into a nervous wreck. When we would read as a group, I would always try to predict when I would be coming up so that I could read over my section to ensure that I knew all the words. As I raced to find the place where I would begin reading, I could feel my heart rapidly beating against my chest, the palms of my hands drenched with sweat, as my mind tried to process what seemed like fifty million thoughts at the same time. There wasn't a calm bone in my body. The anxiety was tremendous, nearly unbearable. I thought that at any moment I was going to pass out.

My worst nightmare became a reality during my ninth grade English class. We were reading Shakespeare. Since we were going in order, I marked where I would start and finish. I quickly read through my part. Although I felt confident that I knew all the words, I was nervous. The longer I read, the more confident I became until I said, "I saw I ... I conquer-ed (kong'quered)." The word is pronounced "kon'kerd." The whole class, including the teacher, burst out laughing. They laughed and laughed. I laughed with them to disguise my embarrassment, but I was dying inside. I was totally humiliated. All the confidence that had risen within me was squashed. At that moment, I hated school and found a reason to dislike the people around me. The truth is that I felt like I had failed myself—again. I wanted the anxiety to stop. I just wanted to be "smart" like everyone else.

My "friends" teased me about that incident throughout high school. And that wasn't the only thing they teased me about. They also called me "monkey paws." I have a friend named Jill to thank for this one. Fate would have it that Jill sat next to me in my English class. She noticed that my hands looked older than I did and brought it to the attention of everyone in the school. In a general conversation with another person, Jill would bring up my hands. She would get the person to look at them and then sing, "Mon-key paws. Mon-key paws." She frequently got a laugh at my expense. I felt like it was her way of separating us, making herself look better than me. For a while it worked.

Even at my cousin's wedding—thirteen years later—Jill brought up my hands. She remembered just how to sing her little song. But this time her taunts didn't hurt because by then I was a fashion and jewelry model for the QVC Network. So no matter what Jill said, I didn't care—and neither did the people around us. They were so enamored with my career choice and having seen me on television, that "monkey paws" was dead and gone. It had lost its power.

Today when I talk with people about being teased, I advise them to just agree with the perpetrator to shut him or her up. It works. It leaves them speechless. You learn that the quickest way to defuse a person is to agree with them even if you know it's not true. It will stop them in their tracks every time. Teasing serves to hurt you. When the person realizes that they can't hurt you, they'll stop. This concept applies also to arguing. A person can't argue with themselves. When you see that the discussion is escalating, just say in your calmest voice, "You're right."

WORDS ONLY HAVE THE POWER YOU GIVE THEM

What I now realize is that "monkey paws" never had any power. It was illusory. Think about it. When did Jill become the expert on defining what are considered attractive or unattractive hands? Did it hurt? Yes, it hurt. Did I sometimes look at my hands and question why they looked as they did? Oh, yeah. And the more she said it, the worse they looked. It really became a mind thing. It made such a great impact on me that years later, while modeling rings during a jewelry show at QVC, I would think about being called "monkey paws." I would even wonder if the "top man" would call down to the producer's desk and pull me off air. Fortunately, it never happened.

I was respected at QVC. I can, however, recall the size of my nose being an issue. The model coordinator suggested that I "shadow my nose." That meant I had a "big" nose and I needed to come up with a solution on how to make it appear slimmer. This required me to darken the sides and lighten the middle. I remember feeling like my status at QVC was in jeopardy because of my "big" nose. I would compare myself to the other girls. I would wonder if I really deserved to be a model or if I was there by chance. Thoughts of doubt swarmed through my head constantly. Thinking that my career would be cut short I would ask myself, "What other talents do you have?" I would even catch myself looking in the preview shot, which is the shot that people in the studio see before it goes online to the viewers, to try and find different ways to angle my face to give it a different appearance.

But my nose was my nose and its size did not change because of the angle. It was what it was and it is what it is. "Here I go again," I thought.

Since I could remember, I had been teased about my "big" nose. My brother had a field day over my nose. He would often make an ugly face, laugh, talk like he had a cold and say, "You have a nose like Granny." Don't get me wrong, I love Granny, but having a replica of her "big" nose wasn't exactly what I had in mind as a way to always remember her. Guys I dated would say, "You've got a big nose." I know that my family loves me, but my nose has been the topic of discussion on many occasions. It seemed I was surrounded by people who noticed my "big" nose. Of course this affected me, but I didn't let it stop me. I had a ten-year career in modeling. Don't let your imperfections stop you.

DON'T PANIC WHEN PEOPLE SAY NEGATIVE THINGS ABOUT YOU

No one can determine your destiny simply by stating their opinion of you—unless you accept their opinion as fact. There is a difference between someone being confident in you and you having confidence in yourself. We have a tendency to be confident because someone puts their confidence in us. But when their confidence in us wavers, we are left with nothing to sustain us. What is of greater value is understanding that someone's confidence in you doesn't determine the outcome. The outcome is determined by your ability to see yourself succeed in your own vision.

My father has shared a story with many young people with the hope of inspiring them to believe in themselves, so I feel comfortable sharing it with you. It's not just a story; it's a true story—one of his many personal journey stories. He was in the eighth grade at sixteen years of age.

Obviously, he wasn't the smartest person in the class. But one day his English teacher asked him a question, to which he didn't have the answer. She responded with, "You are the stupidest boy I have ever seen." From experience, I can imagine the embarrassment and humiliation he must have felt. What about you? Has someone ever said something as stupid as that to you? He says, "I used it to motivate me." He didn't let her words define him.

My dad is now known not only for his work—as one of the best masons in the state of Delaware—but for his humble, gentle, and giving spirit. He has created an amazing life for himself and his family. And he has done it against the odds. As the son of a migrant worker from North Carolina, and the third of nine children, his family moved from state to state working on farms for little pay. They often slept on the ground in chicken houses. My dad never acquired a formal education, but he did understand the importance of a strong work ethic, determination, and personal and spiritual values.

At twenty-one he married my mother, Shirley Maria Taylor, who was just seventeen years old. They were beyond poor, they were "poh"; they lived in a one-bedroom trailer. The bathroom was outside. They ate, slept, and got dressed in the same room. And my mother immediately got pregnant. So now, as my dad puts it, "I didn't know whether to stay or go. I felt like running, but couldn't. I felt like I had taken on more responsibility than I could handle—a wife, a child, and no money." Have you ever felt that way—wanting to avoid a challenge versus face it? Feeling overwhelmed and confused, he talked to God. And God directed my dad. He strengthened him for the mission. My mother stood by his side. Together they worked to build a family and a business. When he was weak, she was strong. When she was weak, he was strong. It wasn't perfect, but it was good. Today, at sixty-five, despite life's challenges, including five children and forty-five years of marriage, my dad still works. And my mother still has his back.

You may be wondering, how does God speak to a person? And how do you know that God is speaking to you when there are many options in life? There are the obvious: through people, meditation, and circumstances. But when you are in a desperate situation, expect the unexpected. This is how my dad learned to read floor plans. After hours of studying his first floor plan he fell asleep at the table overwhelmed, exhausted, and confused. Daddy says that while he was sleeping, he was taught how to read the plan. When he awoke, he had clarity, understanding, and peace.

Everything he saw in his dream was on the floor plan. And he has many similar stories. Whether you believe in God or not, I know that God exists and He is the guiding light and final authority for my journey. You have to determine what will be your guiding light. Even when success wasn't immediately apparent, I would get this unexplainable feeling that I should call certain potential clients. In fact, I called the contact person at DuPont, an international company that is headquartered in Wilmington, Delaware, so many times that he asked me not to call him again. He said, "I'll call you when we need you." Despite his words, when I got that "feeling" again three weeks later I called him. His response? "Renee, I was going to call you today." He booked me on the spot for a photo shoot for their magazine. I have also listened to the feeling when I was knocking on the wrong doors. This meant that I needed to stop wasting my time. Your spirit will guide you, if you let it.

I want to explain the "feeling" because clients always ask me how frequently it comes and how I know it is real. The great philosopher Plato said, "Every living thing carries the breath of God." The feeling is the movement of God's breath through what is called Spirit. Some may refer to it as gut, intuition, or the Holy Spirit. It is one and the same. When it moves, you just know it. Have you ever said, "I knew that was going to happen"? How did you know it was going to happen? It was just a feeling you had, right? That's it. The better you become at listening and following your inner voice, the more fulfilling life you can expect to live.

Each person receives these messages differently. Often, they receive them in more than one way. For some people it is a movement in the belly or in some other part of the body. That is one of the ways I receive messages. It rises up and says, "Here I am. This is for you!" As quick as it comes, it goes. So, I have to be in tune with it. That's how I knew I would be working for United Paramount Network (UPN-57), a television station in Philadelphia. I was scanning through the channels on television. I stopped at a television show called *Studio 57* and the "feeling" was so strong that I knew beyond a shadow of a doubt that I would be hosting that show. Immediately, I called the studio. I didn't get the job until about three months later, but I knew that that was where I was going to be. I didn't know at the time, however, that the current host was thinking about taking a position in Florida. God does not share the details. He makes His move, and then He leaves it up to us to take action. Had I not called, it would have been a missed opportunity.

Some people hear an audible voice. Others, like my father, get messages through a vision or dream. In most cases, every person has more than one way of receiving messages. It doesn't matter how you receive the message. It is important that you listen, as you will receive messages throughout your day. Listening has helped me to discover my truth and uncover the fortunes on my path.

KNOW YOUR VALUE

Your value is far beyond what you see with the natural eye, the people you affiliate with, the car you drive, clothes you wear, and the salary that you earn. And unless you learn how to tap into the spiritual world, you and things around you are just an illusion. One day your unhappiness will confirm that fact. Just look at the many celebrities who "have it all," yet are unhappy and emotionally distraught. Think of all the celebrities who have been addicted to drugs and suffer from other abusive behavior. Clearly, it's not money, fame, and beauty that sets you free! I personally didn't realize how valuable I am until I understood why my purpose is to inspire people to find their own voice in this world. Ever since I was a little girl I had a desire to help people grow into their best selves. But I didn't know why I wanted to help people.

When my purpose and why it was my purpose connected, it was electrifying. My eyes were opened and I knew the worth of my experiences and pain, what I had, why I had it, and what I had to offer because of it. At that moment, everything about my life came into focus.

I had a session with a personal coach. He asked me, "Why do you want to write a book?" I said, "Because I know I can help people." He again asked me, "Why?" I gave another response and the back and forth question and answer period continued for about fifteen minutes. I soon felt the pain of my childhood experiences wallow-up inside of me. The tears began to fall as I shared with him the pain I experienced as a preteen trying to find my place. "I just didn't know where I fit," I explained. "I felt lonely, scared, uncertain, and completely unsure of myself. I hated feeling like that. It was awkward. I was uncomfortable. My classmates teased and taunted me. I felt like an outsider."

These feelings led me to explore personal and spiritual development at a young age. I didn't realize the value of my experiences until my pain met my purpose. At that point, I was liberated. I was able to say goodbye to unfulfilling relationships. I stopped giving people permission to use my time haphazardly. I established my own agenda and called my own shots. I was no longer imprisoned by what others thought of me or what they would or would not do for me. I experienced a calm, serene confidence that I had never experienced before.

It is important for you to understand that your standards and expectations are a reflection of the value you see in yourself. You can only see and use the amount of value that you have released from within. Most people measure their value by how someone feels about them, by what someone else says about them, or by what they do to or for them. This is all deceptive. This means that if they leave them, their value goes with them.

When your value comes from within yourself, it remains steady regardless of what happens. It comes from the abundance found within your soul! It will flow like a river when you understand why you have experienced all that you have and how it connects to your purpose. You must remember that there is value in every thought, feeling, and situation that you experience. There are lessons to learn while seeking love and experiencing pain. Rejection, feelings of hopelessness, mental, emotional, or physical abuse all mean something. It is up to you to figure out what it does mean. Finding your value is like connecting the dots. You have to keep asking yourself why to every question until you get to the emotion or pain of your deepest desires. Once you find the pain or the emotion you'll see the purpose more clearly and why it is your purpose. A confidant or life coach can help you. The clearer your understanding is of your contribution to others, the greater self-value you have.

When you go to a store do you determine the value of products? Of course you do. You don't determine the price, but you do determine whether the price of the item is of equal or greater value to the need that you have for the item. Even when you go to purchase an item whose price is negotiable, the retailer has already determined its value. If the price you offer is below that predetermined value, you're out of luck. Why? Because you offered what the retailer felt was below the products' value.

Let me explain this concept. Our purpose is like a product. It helps solve a problem. The more we understand the problem we solve, the closer we get to our true value. I believe that God is the creator of our purpose, which is according to a perfectly crafted plan. The plan takes into account the universal picture. Every person, situation, and circumstance was thoroughly considered before God determined the purpose and impact that you and I would make. The experiences that we have—when we learn from them--perfects our purpose. But when we fail to learn from our experiences and don't know our purpose it is impossible to know our value. Thereby, never feeling or finding our place of significance.

What would you pay for a product that didn't clearly define how it could benefit you? What would you do with a product that did not have a clearly defined purpose? I have to confess, that I have foolishly purchased items that seemed like a good idea. I was swayed by advertising. But when I got them home, I either didn't like them or see the need for them. So, I threw them in a box and forgot I ever bought them. Yet, how I treated those products is how people treat themselves—and allow others to treat them when they don't know their value.

The fact is that you have been created for a specific and unique purpose. No one else can do what you have been designed and assigned to do. Yes, it's true! God has a plan for your talents, your personality, and your passions. There isn't anything that God placed inside of you that can be taken away by others—unless you surrender it. When you finally recognize your value, you will appreciate and protect it. And you will make choices that reflect that value. Decisions that will lead you to a life of peace and prosperity. Instead of giving your power away to others, you'll retain control of your thoughts and actions. Let me give you an example.

In 1999, I walked into a car dealership. Because I did not know how much value and power my good credit gave me, I drove off the lot not realizing that I could have gotten a much better deal. I overpaid by about $2000. Yes, the salesman took advantage of me, but this costly mistake was entirely my fault. I didn't do my research until after signing the contract. What was I thinking? I then felt cheated and angry. When I was making payments into my fifth and final year, I was still being reminded of the stupid mistake I had made.

Because I didn't assess my value as a consumer, I gave up control to the salesman. I unconsciously gave him the power to determine how much I would pay for the car, the bank I would use to finance the car, and the terms of the loan. The salesman quickly summed me up, and I got cheated. But this won't happen again, because I now know my value as a consumer and I know how to research car costs and value. This shows why self-assessment is so important. It helps you to see, define, and understand your value so that you bring your best to every situation.

I recently saw a guy I graduated from high school with working at the drive-thru window of the local Burger King. He was crying the blues about how rough life was. I shared with him that it would get better, if he changed the way he viewed it. He stepped back from the window and said, "I'll see you later." Obviously, he didn't realize his value. He had made decisions that had led him to a life of frustration and uncertainty. And he had decided that there was nothing he could do to make it better.

TAKE IT EASY, SLOW DOWN, ENJOY THE PROCESS

In life you can have success without value, but you can't have value without success. What do I mean? There are some sports players who are taking steroids, yet they are celebrated for their outstanding athletic abilities. There are businessmen and women who are acquiring wealth at the cost of other's misfortune, yet they are envied for their great financial gain. And there are drug dealers who flaunt their expensive jewelry and fine cars—and in doing so earn the respect of many who want their wealth and power. These individuals have what I call "perceptual success." They have the appearance of success, but we don't see the anxiety that they feel because they live daily with fear, guilt, and shame.

You can have a well-balanced life—spiritually, emotionally, mentally, and financially. Understanding yourself and deciding what you want to stand for in life takes time. If you allow others to pressure you in to doing things that you know you're not ready for, you'll lose a part of yourself and your innocence in the process. Every age has its advantages. As my mother use to say, "If you do everything now, what will be left for you to enjoy and experience later?" If you give yourself permission to embrace each moment of your life as an experience of learning and becoming, you will be giving yourself the best possible chance of having true value and success. Stop telling yourself, "When I grow up I'll..." Enjoy where you are today.

As a teenager I would often say to myself, "When I grow up..." I thought that the adult world was different. I was convinced that if I could just get past these horrible times, life would be perfect. I grew up only to realize that I was so wrong. I was experiencing some of my best moments in life and didn't even realize it. I was so focused on "getting to the better life"—becoming an adult—that I missed the pure, serene joy of growing up. Let me be clear I don't have any desire to be any age: but the age that I am. And I encourage you to appreciate your life at every age as well.

Let me share this secret with you: challenges don't change because you grow up. Get that thought completely out of your head. The circumstances surrounding the challenge may be different, but the core of the challenge is the same. And the wisest solution to any and every problem will always require you to look within yourself for the answer.

Teenagers, young adults, and adults alike deal with peer pressure, gossiping, bickering, relationship issues, self-image concerns, and financial problems. That's why it's important to learn how to best handle challenges now because, I promise you, you'll see them again. Life is like school. You learn, you are tested, and then you see it again. The only thing that is going to make life easier is learning to successfully deal with the everyday realities of life now. I have seen and continue to see some of the same issues I saw five, ten, and fifteen years ago. I'm sure you do, too. You can measure your growth by the outcome you produce. If you keep getting the same results, then do something differently. When you do something different, you will have a different experience and outcome.

In the movie *What the Bleep Do We Know?* the concept was introduced that we react routinely to situations because we are addicted to the chemical that is released in our bodies when we experience certain emotions. For example, falling in love. There is a chemical that is released in our bodies when we feel like we're in love. Some people aren't really in love, they are addicted to the chemical that is released while falling in love. The only way to avoid falling into this trap is to become aware of your choices and why you are making them.

I suggest that you find a mentor. Someone whom you respect, trust, and know has your best interest at heart. Your mentor has to be honest with you. One facet of a mentor's role is to guide you around obstacles. The mentor shares his or her wisdom and knowledge to help you achieve your goals. He or she can hold a mirror up to you, so that you can more objectively see yourself.

DON'T LET REJECTION STOP YOU

Every person has to face and accept rejection throughout his or her life. The important thing is to not take rejection personally. Sometimes your friends don't like you. Your boyfriend doesn't like you or your boss doesn't like you. Some people in the church don't like you. You're not light enough. You're not dark enough. You're not tall enough. You're not short enough. Your hair is too short. Your hair is too long. You're too fat. You're too skinny. None of this is true, because your look is right for your path. You are divinely made for your calling. You're just right for your purpose. So, with the power you have within you, rise above the haters.

My first major head-on collision with rejection came when I was fifteen. I'm not saying this was my first encounter with rejection; just my first major blow. When I was twelve I began developing what I thought would be lifelong friendships with three other girls. We went to house parties together, we shared secrets, we worked at McDonald's together, and we tried to teach each other everything we were learning along the way. Nevertheless, after spending numerous hours talking about boys, sex, tampons, and how to be beautiful, in a single day our friendship ended.

The story is short and simple. These girls came to me and said that they could no longer be my friend because I was black. They said their parents were putting pressure on them to dismiss our friendship. What's amazing is that I was able to deal with losing my best friends. I didn't even spend energy talking about it. I didn't miss a beat. I decided they're entitled to pick their friends and if they want it to be based on color, so be it. It was their loss. I knew that I was a true, loyal friend.

When you overcome rejection, as I did, you lose something and you gain something. In every case, what I gained was so much greater than what I lost. It didn't always feel like it at the time, but when you look for the good you'll find it. This fact gives me comfort in each challenge that I face.

There will be times when it seems that life is demanding more from you than you think you're able to give, but I believe it is God's way of showing us the strength He has placed in us. Most of us can't even conceive of what is in us. And the only way we'll find out is when life throws us a curve ball. It has been said, "When life throws you a lemon make lemonade." The question is, How?

Several years ago, I faced two painful personal rejections within 30 days of one another. My fiancé walked out of my life, and I was fired from my job. That's right, the punches keep coming. But as I have, you can handle it. And how you handle the challenge is as important as the challenge itself. Learn all you can from each one, because the last challenge will build your skills to handle the next one.

Prior to getting engaged, I firmly stated that we would not set a date until we went to marriage counseling. Not just counseling with a minister, but with a counselor who would tell us more than just pray about it. I thought we had some serious issues that required concrete answers. That does not mean I don't believe in prayer, because I do. But I also understand that ministers and church folk across this country are walking through the doors of divorce court and calling it quits.

Clearly, marriage requires prayer and a strategic plan. And I wasn't going to have one without the other. My fiancé and I had an argument about going to counseling. The disagreement didn't catch me by surprise. The truth is that although we enjoyed each other, we had our fair share of challenges to overcome; challenges that getting married would not solve. You'll notice that before situations arise in your life, there are warning signs all around you. A wise person will stop, listen, and respond accordingly. My former fiancé asked me to marry him and four months later walked out of my life. I haven't had a conversation with him since.

In the September 18, 2003, edition of *USA Today*, there was an article published about Ben Affleck and Jennifer Lopez's decision to postpone their wedding. The reason is none of our business. In the article, University of Washington sociologist Pepper Schwartz was quoted as saying, "Hollywood would like to say it's the general jitters, but in a mature relationship, you really ought to have worked everything out before you set a wedding date. The wedding itself should be a party, an event, a way to get dishes, whatever it is." As written in the article, "jitters should be confined to other anxieties: How many people are coming? Will the food show up?" I couldn't have said it better.

In less than 30 days after my fiancé walked out of my life, I was fired from my job. I was being bullied by my supervisor—humiliated in front of my staff, described as a premadonna, and told I couldn't write. I was the director of public relations at my alma mater, Delaware State University (DSU). It was a challenging and exciting time in my life. After seeking help from the director of human resources and the university president, I was granted medical leave due to the tremendous amount of stress that they knew I was experiencing. The stress affected my health. I went to the doctor who diagnosed me as being depressed. He prescribed an antidepressant. Yes, I felt like my life was crumbling out of control, but everything about my life up to this point told me that God had prepared me for this personal and professional challenge.

Despite feeling alone, scared, and hurt, I threw the antidepressants in the trash, made up my mind that my life was going to change, and began my journey back to myself by closely guarding what I fed my mind and who I affiliated with. When I returned to work two weeks later, the president told me that they would not be renewing my contract and that effective December 31 I would no longer be employed. My self-esteem went to its lowest point ever. I remember wondering how it got to this point. I was a student of developing and maintaining a positive self-image. I taught others how to develop and maintain theirs. What happened? I was numb. I couldn't feel myself anymore. I was deaf to my own voice. All I could hear were the people in my personal and professional life whose actions were saying, "You're not good enough." I was now a student of my own teaching.

Everything that I had learned over the years about connecting with God, confidence, winning, and persevering I retrieved from my spirit. I would sit on the floor in my bedroom, look myself in the mirror, and with a river of tears streaming down my face, would painfully scream for Renee like she was in another room. I would wrap my arms around myself and remind myself of how much she was loved and that she would rise again. I didn't know where she was, but my sole purpose every day was to find her. Day after day when I woke up I would jump out of bed and run to the mirror hoping to see her. Before I went to bed I would say to her, "I'll see you in the morning." During the day, I would pretend that she had it all together.

I wasn't pretending because of people. I knew that it was my fight and only I had the weapons to win. I didn't talk about it. I just fought with prayer, affirmation, and the vision that God had already shown me for my life. It was all I had. Yes, my mother, father and other earthly angels tried to reach me, but I was in a place that only God and I could go. And I'm so thankful that He was there. The pain was so deep that I couldn't win the battle with external stuff and people. It was there, in that place, that I found that *There Is More Inside.*

In the end, I was asked to sign a letter of resignation, which was written by someone in the president's office. I refused to sign it, and left with a renewed surge of energy and optimism for my future. The president was impressed with my ability to be positive despite the circumstances. What he didn't know was that I decided a long time ago that rejection was only a part of refining my character—not defining my direction.

LEARN THE LESSON AND GET ON WITH LIFE

The journey back to myself didn't end there. It continued for nearly two years. I had to rebuild, reshape, and refocus. When I finally came out I was better, stronger, and wiser than ever before. I definitely had a new perspective about who Renee was and where she was going.

What did the events of 2001 teach me? Four very significant lessons that I would like to share with you. First, understand the meaning of "To thine own self be true." You have to listen to your own heart. No one can decide what is best for you. Do not *ever* surrender who you really are to anyone. And always value and appreciate yourself more than you expect others to value and appreciate you. Let your power be internal, not external.

Second, don't let people say anything they want to you. Every word that a person speaks to you will strengthen or weaken you. If you find that a person is trying to break you, don't play Russian roulette with that person. Let your position be known in a firm and fair way, and that in no uncertain terms your self-esteem will not be tampered with. And tell them that the way they are speaking to you is unacceptable. If necessary, move on to another department within the organization or to another company altogether. And if it's your love interest, drop him or her like a hot potato. Your self-esteem is the lifeline to your happiness and freedom. Do not give it to anyone.

Third, don't be angry. Anger will only block positive forces from moving in your life. Letting go of anger is rejuvenating. Freeing yourself of it will bring clarity, creativity, and power to your life. When situations come into our lives, they serve a greater purpose than we can ever imagine.

It's also important to note that we invite most of these situations into our lives either consciously or unconsciously. So, take responsibility. Don't hold up the process by housing negative energy. Don't be angry with people or yourself. Simply step back, look at yourself, learn the lesson, and move on.

One of golf guru Tiger Woods' secrets to success is his ability to look at himself and take full responsibility for everything that happens on the golf course. According to Tiger, he learned to take responsibility for what happens from both his parents. He said, "When I hit a bad shot, my dad used to say to me: "Who hit that shot? Was it the club? Was it the ball?" Like Tiger, taking responsibility gives you power to become great.

Finally, know that God has your back. Let me give you an example. My last day at the University was December 31, 2001. On January 2, 2002, just two days later, I went back to being self-employed. By the end of March 2002, I had signed my first contract with the state of Delaware and the April issue of *Delaware Today* was on the stands. *Delaware Today* is Delaware's premiere magazine. I was featured on the cover as one of "40 Delawareans under 40" to watch. By June, I was promoting Delaware's largest antipoverty agency and the rewards were significant. Like me, as you look back over your life, you'll see that God has done miraculous things for you when you least expect it. I don't know the mind of God and neither do you. So, don't let rejection stop you!

YOU ARE PERFECT FOR YOUR PURPOSE

How do I know this? By experiencing success in an industry where I was first rejected by the "experts." In most cases, being a model requires height and beauty. I wasn't blessed with a lot of either. But I persisted because I knew I was on purpose. What do I mean? The answer has two parts. Part One, "I knew who I was." I understood my core character. I knew my values, talents, and best qualities. Part Two, I believed in my dream.

Growing up, everyone has a dream. Isn't there something that makes you think that you could make a difference in this world? Your gut tells you that if you were able to do it, you would be fulfilled. You don't know how it can happen, but you know that it's possible because it grips you every time you think about it.

As you experience life and talk to people who make negative, insecure statements, walls are built around your dream. After a while you can't see your dream, only the walls of doubt that say, "I can't do this," "People who are successful are smarter than me," and "I don't fit." Successful people have these thoughts too, but they know that all the necessary provisions have been made to make their dreams come true, despite other people's limited vision. They simply take life an experience at a time. The difference between you and the people that you admire is faith and courage. Their faith gives them the courage to move forward despite their doubts.

You have to believe in yourself. You have to know what your heart is telling you. You have to work hard. You have to knock on doors. And more doors. And work harder. You must ignore people who express their limited opinion of you. In the past, I would mentally and verbally cancel limiting statements people spoke to me so that it wouldn't enter my subconscious and stop me from pursuing my dreams. It went like this: "I don't receive that. I will overcome. Someone will give me an opportunity."

I know it is difficult living in a world that puts a heavy burden on people to be perfect. And not just perfect, but perfect according to a specific standard. Make it easy for yourself. Always do and be your best, whatever that is at the time, and leave the rest to God. If He can't do it, it can't be done. And you don't need the pressure. According to the American Society of Plastic Surgeons, which represents 97 percent of America's board-certified plastic surgeons, the top five procedures for women between the ages of nineteen and thirty-four in 2004 were breast augmentation (130,700), nose reshaping (113,026) liposuction (90,969), tummy tuck (25,684) and breast lift (21,983). Nose reshaping and breast augmentation were also among the top five in the eighteen and younger age group. There were nearly 1.5 million surgical procedures performed among these groups. That's a lot of young people who are unhappy with how they look. I would guess that a survey of people's discontentment with their physical features would reveal even more startling numbers.

What I think people fail to realize is that when they seek the perfection of Halle Berry, Jennifer Lopez, and Tyra Banks they are seeking the impossible. It's a false image. Are they beautiful? Absolutely! Are they perfect? Absolutely not. What many people also fail to take in to account is that they will never be able to attain this external beauty because much of it resides inside these women. Their beauty is deeper than what we see. It's a package. It is who they are. It's the untouchable that makes them who they are.

I see beautiful women every day. Some are as beautiful as those just mentioned, but because of their internal stuff they go unnoticed. My sister-in-law, who crossed over in 1998, was one of the most beautiful women I had ever seen. I would tell her that she should model, but she didn't have the confidence. At times, I would work with her on her walking, but to no avail. No matter how much I believed in her, she needed to believe in herself.

Stop thinking about plastic surgery, dieting, and perfection and start thinking purpose, power, and destiny. I'm not saying that you shouldn't eat healthy and work on how you present yourself. What I am saying is that some of you are giving yourself grief for no reason. You're perfect for the purpose that you're here to serve. God has given you all you need.

As you grow to know, understand, and love yourself, you will realize that perfection, as defined by society, is the least of your worries. Primarily because you'll realize it is unobtainable. Don't be confused; excellence is a reasonable goal. Think about this. Beauty obviously isn't the safeguard to a life of bliss. Just read newspapers, magazines, or watch television interviews with Angelina Jolie, Halle Berry, Jennifer Lopez, and many other talented, beautiful women. They are, just like you and me, trying to find the secret to a monogamous, genuinely happy relationship. Clearly, being externally beautiful is not the secret. Mature men understand that women in magazines and on television are made to appear perfect. The key word is appear. You would be amazed what the right lighting, makeup, photographer, and touch-up artist can do for you. I have a picture of myself that every time someone sees it they exclaim, "Is that you? That doesn't look like you!" I smile and say, "Nice lighting, a phenomenal makeup artist, and the photographer is the best in Philadelphia." Magazines and television create fantasy. That's their purpose. People with a positive self-image accept that fact. If you're measuring yourself by the images and information that you see and hear in the media, without question building and maintaining a positive self-image will be your greatest challenge. It is not all about external beauty! *There Is More Inside.*

A POSITIVE SELF-IMAGE DOESN'T MEAN YOU'RE GOING TO BE PERFECT

A positive self-image doesn't fully eliminate the impulse to question yourself. Nor does it lead you into a mistake-free life of bliss and merry. Being human guarantees that you will make mistakes. But that's okay. Having a positive self-image does, however, give you permission to trust and act on your own judgment. Because we sometimes make mistakes by not trusting ourselves, we lose faith in ourselves. But maturity teaches us how to quickly bounce back and responsibly live with our decisions. That's why living is a daily process. The best part about making a mistake is that it's not a mistake at all, only a learning experience. You can change, alter, or reverse any decision—not necessarily the situation—but the decision. You have the power!

Take a moment to think about and write down your response to the following statements.

11. When I think about myself, I think most often about...

_____

_____

12. It makes me feel good when...

_____

_____

13. It hurts when people say...

_____

_____

14. I know that what people say about me isn't true because...

_____

_____

15. It is most important that I...

_____

_____

16. I think most about becoming...

_____

_____

Chapter 3

DECISION MAKING:
IT'S ALL UP TO YOU

I had to accept responsibility for abandoning my values.
I separated myself from the true source of love.
I was innocent, but I wasn't naive.

You've heard it over and over again. Where a person is in their life today, represents the choices they've made along the way. When I first heard this concept it seemed pretty simple to me. It made perfect sense. If I made the right choices, I would have a happy, fulfilled life. If I made the wrong choices it could be disastrous. Notice I said choices, not choice, because we are continually making choices. And there isn't just one choice that leads to disaster, but a series of choices. Perhaps looking at it this way will help. Your choices should lead you to the picture (vision) you have for your life. When you are presented with a choice, it will either lead you to or further away from your vision. Each choice is a piece to the puzzle — either it fits in order to complete the picture — or it doesn't.

Don't let anyone tell you that there are free choices because there aren't. Every choice has a price tag. Some are more costly than others. And every decision will affect your self-esteem, self-respect, or reputation one way or the other. Some decisions may cause you to win or lose financially. And still others may have a health consequence.

WHAT'S YOUR GUARANTEE?

As we listen to the testimonies of people who have beaten drug and alcohol addiction, bad marriages, and other wrong turns, it might seem that if we choose to take the wrong path, we only have to turn around to fix our lives. Unfortunately, it's not that easy. Often times there aren't quick fixes to the problems we create. And many people don't get that chance because they lose their life while on the wrong path. They literally die in the fight.

A counselor told me that only one percent of teenagers make a comeback from drug and alcohol abuse. Only 10 percent of adults are able to do so. According to the National Institute of Alcohol Abuse and Alcoholism, U.S. adolescents who begin drinking before age fifteen are four times more likely to develop alcohol dependence than those who begin drinking at age twenty-one. It is estimated that over three million teenagers are alcoholics. On college campuses alcohol abuse accounts for 500,000 injuries, 600,000 assaults, and 70,000 sexual assaults. Tragically, alcohol is the leading factor in the cause of death among 15 to 24-year-olds. The top three causes of death in Americans of this age are homicides due to automobile accidents, suicides, and dependence on alcohol and other drugs.

These statistics are startling and very sad. And it's even more disturbing when it's your family member. I have a friend whose mother and sister were killed by drunken drivers eighteen years apart. Both drivers were under the age of twenty-five. The young lady who killed her sister was on probation for drunken driving. This is a tremendous loss for anyone to suffer. As I have seen her struggle to come to grips with the senseless murder of her loved ones, I find it troubling how our society sometimes carelessly responds to alcohol abuse.

For example, in 2004, before being named Miss Delaware USA 2005, this certain young lady—after falling asleep at the wheel of her car—

pleaded guilty for drunken driving. While still on probation in November 2004, she was named Miss Delaware USA 2005. After it was brought to the attention of the national pageant organizers, they had to decide if she would remain Miss Delaware USA. In justifying their decision to allow her to keep the title, a Miss USA Pageant spokesperson said, "What 22-year-old hasn't done that?" I'm not judging their decision, however, the reasoning behind the decision is shocking. It sends the message that every present or former twenty-two-year-old has committed the crime of driving while intoxicated. That simply isn't true!

What may seem like an innocent experiment becomes, for many, a dark shadow that they can't walk away from. Nothing can convince me that anyone intends to become addicted to and die from alcohol or drug abuse. A friend, who was an alcoholic for nearly twenty years, took his first drink at fifteen during a church conference. He didn't stop until he went to Alcoholics Anonymous meetings. Although extremely intelligent and talented, he was unable to complete college or sustain a job or marriage due to the abuse. He has been sober for nearly a decade, and has been working to get his life back on track.

I don't believe alcoholics want to be alcoholics. I think that when you make decisions that get you so far out, your state of mind changes. At that point, it becomes very difficult to connect with your inner strength, to loosen the grip of the addiction. My logic is that your mind has created the habit of listening to the addiction versus listening to yourself. The longer you silence yourself, the harder it is to hear your own voice. Please be clear, I'm not saying it can't be done. I know firsthand from watching family and friends struggle, that it is a very difficult journey.

I witnessed this struggle when one of my mother's siblings died in 1993 after abusing drugs and alcohol. He was only forty-eight years old. This relative repeatedly made bad decisions. He was in and out of prison. He abandoned his children and he chose to hustle on the streets. However, on numerous occasions, he tried to make a comeback. He got married and had what looked like a picture-perfect family. He tried different spiritual paths, including Christianity and Islam. He tried leaving the streets and connecting with people who were living a different lifestyle. But he continued to struggle. He is one of millions who never made a successful comeback because they don't know that *There Is More Inside*.

GET FOCUSED AND STAY ON TRACK!

People get off track for four primary reasons. The first is peer pressure, the second is the lack of discipline and focus, the third is the lack of clearly defined values, and the fourth is understanding personal accountability. Let's look at peer pressure.

As I remember being a teenager and young adult, it was obvious from the decisions that my friends and I were making that most of us were scared, lacked confidence, and were simply following the crowd. What's really scary is that there are adults who still allow peer pressure to be a factor in their decision making. Most of the time I was a leader, but I had my moments of following, too.

For instance, I can remember one time when I was at a youth church conference in Bermuda. I was about fifteen years old. Everyone was smoking cigarettes and they keep pressuring me to smoke. The more I said no, the more they insisted. They made me feel like I was a nerd by not participating. So, I lit up. They laughed and said, "You didn't inhale." At that moment, I really felt silly and nerdish. They made me think that if I did what they did they would accept me, but they still made fun of me. I couldn't please them. Their minds were made up. To them, I just wasn't cool. It didn't matter what I would do to try to change their perception; they were simply trying to make a fool of me. And that's exactly what they did because I felt like a fool; I looked like a fool, because I was being a fool. I felt like I had stepped out of my skin and I was looking at myself saying, "What the heck are you doing? You don't smoke!" There I was standing in a hotel conference room at a church conference wearing a pink dress with white polka dots trying to smoke a cigarette for the first time because someone dared me to. I was a real class act—NOT!

According to information provided by the American Academy of Child and Adolescent Psychiatry and the National Institute of Drug Abuse teens who smoke are three times more likely to use alcohol, eight times more likely to use marijuana, and twenty-two times more likely to use cocaine. Smoking is also associated with other risky behaviors, such as fighting and having unprotected sex. After my smoking experience, I went back to saying no to anything and anybody who asked me to participate in something that I didn't believe in.

Soon after I made that commitment to myself my values were put to the test. Values—you know—the personal philosophy a person has about life and living. I was at a pool party and my brother's friend, who I had a crush on for several years, was there. He was eighteen years old. I was fifteen. I can't remember anyone swimming because nearly everyone had found a drinking and sex partner. Everyone except me. I really wanted to leave, but I had caught a ride with someone else. There I was sitting alone and feeling lonely and awkward. I must confess that although drinking and sex weren't on my mind, there was a hidden desire for someone to show me attention, too.

From across the room, he read my mind. He came over and we talked. He was drinking and offered me some of what he was having. Although tempted to say yes so that I would appear mature to him, I declined. The conversation was stimulating and his attention was flattering. It made me feel attractive. Our conversation continued and out of complete surprise to me, he took my hand and started leading me. I didn't know where we were going. My heart starting pounding. I began to question within myself, "What is he doing? Where are we going?" We reached the bathroom and he quickly closed the door and immediately pulled me close to him. He started kissing me. This felt so wrong, yet I didn't say anything. It was happening so fast that it seemed like the moment never came for me to tell him that I was uncomfortable and that there was a misunderstanding.

As we continued to kiss, I felt him slowly push my body to the floor. My mind was still stuck on, "What is he doing?" We were on the floor and he was on top. As we were kissing, his hand reached for my belt buckle. My eyes swiftly opened and my mind snapped to attention. His eyes were still closed. I was thinking about everything all at once! "Who is this man on top of me?" "My parents will kill me if I get pregnant!" Everything that my brother Joe told me about boys rose up within me. "This is disgusting," I thought. "He'll tell everybody at school if I have sex with him. This isn't the way I want to have sex. He should love me and I should love him. I want to wait until I'm married. I barely know him!"

Suddenly, I pushed him back and said, "I don't want to have sex with you." He whispered some miscellaneous comfort words and continued fumbling for my belt buckle. In my most firm, confident voice I said, "STOP! I don't want to have sex with you!" He got up, didn't say one word and left the bathroom. I stayed in the bathroom for a while looking myself in the mirror. I didn't know how or what to feel. I kept asking myself, "What just happened? Oh my God, what just happened?"

When I connected with Renee, I smiled at myself and quietly celebrated the confidence that rose up within me to say no. Later that evening, he locked himself in a room with another girl. I now realize I put myself in a dangerous situation. He could have ignored my request to stop.

That never happened again. In order to stand my ground, I had to exercise discipline and focus. At all the parties I've attended—as a teenager and adult—where drugs, alcohol, and sex were readily available, having a plan of action empowered me to say no. In most cases, I left. And at other times I just said, no. Instead of being concerned with what others were doing, I thought about and focused on what I wanted for my life. A friend of mine wasn't so lucky. She lost her virginity and self-esteem while at a party.

There are two sides to this story—hers and theirs. She says she was drunk and doesn't remember. The guys say that she was alert and agreed to their proposition. Regardless, my friend was devastated to realize that after a night of binge drinking she had sex with two guys in one night. What was supposed to be a secret wasn't a secret for long. In the midst of her internal struggle, her insecurities magnified. She got pregnant during her freshman year in college and dropped out. She left her baby with her mother and continued living her life on the run. She now realizes that you can't run from yourself.

Many people get into trouble because they forget about personal accountability. They focus so much on being accepted that they momentarily forget that there are consequences to every choice that they make. They say to themselves, "I'm going to try crack just this one time." Maybe, at a party where "everybody was doing it," they try marijuana. Comedians often joke about how people act while passing a joint around —as each person squints their eyes, they tighten their lips and inhale. It seems funny until they begin to lose control over their lives. When they begin to live for the next high. When it becomes the way they spell relief from day-to-day realities. When drinking, popping pills, or getting high becomes the ultimate relief of the day. When they can no longer look themselves in the mirror and love what they've become.

As friends, parties, and peer pressure increase so does the unanticipated pressure to keep up. Some people want to escape. They realize that they're in over their head, but they feel like they have to save face. Saying no takes courage, strength, and confidence. Unfortunately, the moment they say "yes" when they really want to say "no" they've already surrendered all three. And each time, "yes" becomes easier.

It's not until they've lost their peace of mind, their joy, sense of family, and their self-respect that they realize the worth of personal value. But by then, it seems unattainable and the person feels unworthy. The only thing that matters is getting high; escaping to that place where they can feel emotionally pain-free. They become cowards! There's nothing funny about drugs. Ask my former co-worker who started out as a "seller, not a user." She promised herself that she would never use drugs, as she saw what it was doing to others, but one day on her way to Philly with some "friends" for a drug drop, she was talked into trying marijuana. This was the start of her experimenting with marijuana and crack and everything in the middle. She separated herself from the love of God, herself, her family, and friends. She says, "I just couldn't face them in the state that I was in. I had no self-worth. I felt like I deserved what was happening to me." You can tell yourself that that won't happen to you. You can say, "Mmmm, she was weak." You can think that you're stronger than that and that your ability to earn a high school diploma, get accepted into college, and secure a corporate position gives you special immunity from addiction. But you better think twice. Many people think the same thing until it happens to them.

I remember a friend who was so addicted to marijuana that he didn't know his five-year-old daughter was watching him get high through the crack in the door. He didn't know until she told him that she saw him light up one of those "funny cigarettes" in the bathroom. Clearly, his uncontrollable addiction and inability to face the day-to-day challenges took precedence over his love for himself and his daughter.

Your state of mind when you try any type of chemical will determine how you react to it. If you're not in the right place mentally, emotionally, spiritually, and physically, you don't know where that path might take you. And if you would consider trying drugs, you are not in the right state of mind.

When a person makes the choice to abuse drugs and alcohol, he or she loses touch with who he or she really is. People who abuse their bodies and minds will eventually lose control over their lives, their priorities and their goals. Their purpose naturally derails. The addiction doesn't have to be drugs. It can be anything that has priority over what's in their best interest. Addiction is easily recognized because it controls our behavior. It argues with our conscience and robs us of common sense. It doesn't matter what it is; addiction talks and thinks faster than we do. Its sole purpose is to silence our voice so that we can't hear ourselves anymore. As we gasp for air, fighting to live, we lie to ourselves with every breath. We make excuses. The only problem is, our spirit won't respond; it refuses to lie to us. This combination creates conflict within us. It never gives us peace. We would give anything to stop the internal battle by silencing one voice or another.

My integrity has been challenged many times over the course of my life. And it continues to be. I've been asked to fire someone undeservingly, entertain married men who were coming in from out of town for business, and be a mistress in exchange for a talk show opportunity. I know and understand peer pressure first-hand. But it comes down to choice. You can stand up and be accountable for yourself or you can listen to everyone else and crack under the pressure.

Knowing my values and having faith in my dreams have saved me. If you want to have the strength to stand up to peer pressure, have discipline and focus, live your values, and be accountable for yourself—have a vision for your life! If people are doing things around you that conflict with your values or move you further away from your plan, simply walk away. Build relationships with people who have common goals. This will create an unbelievable synergy, which means that you are more powerful and effective with someone else or a group than you are by yourself.

For two years I worked with a college football team on their personal and professional development. I had one huge challenge: each player had to understand the role he played in the team's success. Each player was making minute-by-minute choices that were affecting his personal and professional life, and the team's overall performance. Each player needed to understand that he was responsible for his own choices. If he couldn't make the right decisions off the field, despite his natural athletic ability on the field, his poor decision-making skills would catch up with him. And as you read the headlines about collegiate and pro sports players, for many of them it does. Good decision makers create the habit of making good decisions.

The mind operates on experience. When forced to make a quick decision, the mind and body work on impulse. It will make the decision based on what it knows. Reacting is allowing your emotions to dictate your course of action. When you respond, you let a thought process guide your actions. When you are put under pressure and a quick decision is required, your mind works on impulse and your body works on reflex. So, the best way to become a good decision maker is to get in the habit of making good decisions.

THE CHOICE REALLY IS YOURS

Sometimes we forget that our life is in our own hands. And that no matter what anyone else is doing, we are accountable for what we do. We know what we should do, but it isn't what we want to do, so we go around asking others what we should do until we find someone that gives us the answer we want the hear. Then we have an excuse to do what we want to do although it's exactly what we shouldn't do. For a brief time, during my mid-twenties, I mistakenly convinced myself—because I wanted to—that I was okay even though I knew what I was doing was wrong. Of course, like most people, I had identified someone else to blame for my actions. I have since learned that when we hurt we try to heal through others. Instead of taking time out for ourselves to connect with our internal strength, we dangerously seek healing through someone else. I chose this incredibly self-deprecating path of deception. After being in several physically and emotionally abusive relationships, and finding out that men whom I loved and trusted violated their marriage vows, I thought that I could protect myself by being the other woman. Let me be clear, married men were never my target. As far as I'm concerned, married men are off limits. In fact, if a man is in any kind of committed relationship he is off limits. But I decided to be flexible with my values simply because I stopped believing in love.

Disappointed over failed relationships, my own and others, I found myself unconsciously seeking fulfillment in non-committed sexual relationships. I didn't intentionally target men with girlfriends. But even after it became clear that there was another person in the picture—although they were not married—I didn't immediately make a decision to call it quits. These were not long-term relationships, but I didn't do what I knew my heart was telling me to do—to end it immediately!

I had to accept responsibility for abandoning my values. I separated myself from the true source of love. I was innocent, but I wasn't naïve. It became clear to me that I was creating a pattern that would eventually lead to complete spiritual and/or physical death. Deepak Chopra, the author of *The Seven Spiritual Laws of Success,* says that our relationship with others is a reflection of the relationship that we have with ourselves. Even prior to reading that profound statement, I realized that my actions had nothing to do with the men I got involved with. It was all about me and my hurt. The moment I stopped believing in love, I stopped believing in God.

Internally, I was going through life trying to digest why people commit adultery or "mess around." Because I couldn't get a grasp on immorality and this issue in particular, it plagued me. It absorbed so much of me that I judged, yet lived a life from the very issue that taunted me. My life mirrored my internal battle. Your life mirrors your internal battle. It's not about the people who are driving you crazy; it is about the internal issues that are taunting you.

What do I mean? In life, we often find ourselves blaming others for what's happening to us. But we subconsciously create whatever is in our lives through our thoughts that determine our actions. In my case, I couldn't blame the men that I was involved with. At that time, I was being taunted by my own insecurities. So, I felt safer as the "other woman." Have your fears ever caused you to desert your values? You know what is right, but it seems safer to do the opposite? Take it from me, it's not worth it! Face your fears and live your destiny!

It is difficult and embarrassing for me to admit this, but I violated the relationship of another couple. And even though they were *not* married, they were still a couple. Of even higher significance, I violated the relationship I had with myself. Fortunately, I realized that I had to make a decision for the person that I had to face in the mirror every day; a decision that would determine my future and how I saw myself. I returned to my values and reaffirmed my commitment to being unattached to anyone unless I was the one and only.

Meeting someone and bringing them into your life is like hiring for a job. Unfortunately, a lot of people don't know exactly what type of employee they are looking for. They begin the interviewing process anyway with hopes of finding the perfect candidate. When applicants come in, you simply ask them what they bring to the table. Based on what you hear, one candidate seems especially impressive. She is flawless with her presentation skills. She's attractive, well dressed, personable, and an excellent communicator. She is an active participant in the interview. She answers your questions well, and she asks all the right questions. Her listening skills are as good as her speaking skills. She also expresses high moral standards. After spending about an hour with her, you admit she's just the person you're looking for. With her background and skills, you're afraid you might lose her to another employer, so you make an offer at the highest salary you can afford.

In the beginning, the new employee shows great promise. She arrives on time and stays late. Her ability to act independently with a fresh approach really moves you. She meets deadlines and never complains about the amount of responsibility she has or what it takes to please you. Your time together is extremely satisfying. You can't imagine how you ever lived without her. A few months pass and you notice she has begun to arrive a few minutes late. After a few more months, she begins to call in sick. She becomes defensive when you express concern about her unusual behavior. As time passes she becomes less reliable. You can't understand it. You try to justify it. You do everything except admit to yourself that you moved too fast and made the wrong choice. Does this sound familiar? This is what I've learned.

First, you should know the type of person you are looking to bring into your life. Second, take time to get to know them. Talk, talk, and talk some more. Don't give them all that you have upfront. Let them make an investment too. Give him or her the opportunity to back up all the wonderful things that he or she has stated about him or herself. Do more listening than talking. Third, spend time with his or her family and friends. Observing them together will tell you a lot about them. Fourth, grow to love the person and give them an opportunity to love you. Remember, what you sell the person is what they will buy. So if you sell the person on your money, great sex, or lifestyle, don't get mad when that's what the person falls in and out of love with.

ELIMINATING FEAR-BASED DECISIONS

For most of us, fear has directed our lives for as long as we can remember. "Stop before you fall and hurt yourself," mothers often warn. "Fear the Lord, for He is great," exclaim preachers. "If you don't give me your ice cream, I'm going to kick your butt after school," warns the bully. "If you don't do this with me, I'm not going to be your friend," claims a manipulative friend. "Are you sure you want to be a doctor? You're going to have to go to school seven more years after college," warns the underachiever.

I'm confident that you can create your own list of warnings that have caused you to resort to making what I call fear-based decisions. These are decisions that are based on obstacles, insecurities, and past negative experiences. Instead of claiming our right to our unlimited blessings, abilities, and talents, we allow past experiences and people who are driven by fear to influence and ultimately rob us of our best.

Often, when working with people on identifying and facing their fears, I ask them what they want to achieve and what's stopping them from doing so. What I've consistently found is fear. What you need to know is that in every case that I can think of, the fear was illusory. I'm not saying that there aren't genuine concerns or challenges that we need to take into consideration when we make a decision. What I am saying, however, is that when you get right down to it, there isn't anything stopping you from achieving your goals—except you. Remember that courage is simply doing what you fear.

Have you ever observed a child who is on the verge of taking his or her first step? It is with anticipation and confidence that he will walk. Although the child doesn't have the complete understanding of how to walk, he makes the effort. He takes the first step. He falls. He gets up again. He takes a step. He falls. He gets up again. And determinedly takes a step. Fear doesn't stop him because he hasn't yet learned to use it as an excuse.

When you look closely at obstacles in your life, choose to see them like that baby does. What you'll learn from your attempts is the bridge needed for your success. After all, every mistake that we make gives us understanding and clarity that leads to greatness. I admit that it took way too long for me to learn that mistakes are okay. Eventually, however, understanding the power of mistakes gave me the freedom to explore life more fully. I don't know any successful person who did it right the first time. The easiest thing to do is to give up on your dreams when it gets tough, to turn around, and go in another direction.

When I was young I was extremely shy and timid: I was literally scared of my own shadow. In fact, my father nicknamed me "Ninny," which according to the Webster's Dictionary, means a foolish and weak person. Although he didn't know what it meant, it caught on quickly. I admit that I earned the nickname. I was scared of the dark. I had nightmares about animals being under my bed. I secretly was uncomfortable going in stores, and I didn't feel right being around strangers. Simply put, I was anxious about everything!

But one of the people who looked past my fears to see greatness within me was the director of Christian Education at my church. This God-fearing woman played a major role in my personal development. She challenged me to be better. She rewarded me when I was successful. She praised me for opening my mouth and speaking. She saw leadership skills in me and encouraged me to lead. She pushed me to the front. And when I needed to be put in my place, she did so with love and wisdom. Because of her devotion and love for developing young people, I developed a passion for the stage. I could make mistakes in the church and still be applauded for my effort. This support encouraged me to try again and again. Eventually, the passion for speaking and expressing myself came to life and here I am today, still pursuing my real dream. And my dad no longer calls me "Ninny"!

MAKING DESTINY-DIRECTED DECISIONS

Do you have childhood dreams that you're not embracing because you're afraid? As a young girl I pretended to be a television star. In my daydreams, I even won an Emmy! Although I worked to develop skills in acting and public speaking, I didn't dare share my dream with anyone. I protected it and hid it in my heart.

In high school I heard my peers begin to stake claims to their purpose in life. They would confidently say, "I'm going to be a doctor." "I'm going to be a teacher." "I'm going to be a lawyer." I didn't want to be the only person without direction, but as I listened to my peers, I began to feel perplexed and lonely. I said to myself, "I'm the only person who doesn't have the foggiest idea as to what she can realistically become in life." It seemed like everyone else had it all together. While I felt like a lost puppy that couldn't find her way home, I later learned that there were a lot of other students unsure of what to become too. What stupid reason compelled us to act like we had it all together? What was wrong with saying, "I don't know," "I'm scared," "I don't have all the answers," or "Will you help me?"

Instead, we lived by the phrase, "Fake it until you make it." We selected colleges because they were out of state or because they impressed our friends and family. Like many of my friends, I fell into this trap. For image sake, I declared I was going to be a lawyer. It was a "SMART" goal, which stands for Specific, Measurable, Attainable, Realistic and Target Date. I picked Hampton University, although I knew absolutely nothing about Hampton University except that it was in Virginia. So, although I harbored other dreams in my heart, I now had an answer for the frequently asked question, "What do you want to be when you grow up?"

I could breathe deeply, put my shoulders back, hold my head high and say, "A lawyer." People were impressed. They were also impressed by my choice of school. "You'll fit right in down there," they said. I was scared by their encouragement. Every time a person would say anything positive about my choice, I would secretly hope that they would offer me some insight into what being a lawyer really meant.

What I now realize is that when adults ask, "What do you want to be when you grow up?" they aren't really expecting a young adult to firmly know the answer. Most adults know that the majority of college graduates will not work in the occupation that they choose to study. I had a friend who also said she was going to be a lawyer. We even made plans to go to law school together. Guess what? I'm not a lawyer and neither is she! As I sat in my required pre-law courses, I felt like I was dying of boredom! I didn't want to be a lawyer. I wanted to be on television!

Although that dream still seemed out of reach, when I saw the Oprah Winfrey Show for the first time, I said, out loud "I want to do that!" Oprah was doing what I had been imagining for years. She was changing people's lives through the message of personal accountability and positive thought. That was it. My heart had spoken. Yet, fear quickly silenced my inner voice with words of logic. It regulated my thoughts. For instance, I wasn't remotely close to the entertainment industry. I didn't know anyone in the business. I didn't know how to travel in New York or Philadelphia by myself. In order to get what I wanted, I had to overcome my fears and embrace adventure.

I also told my parents about my dreams. I told them that I thought one way to get there was to pursue a career in modeling. I thought my mother would have a heart attack. She couldn't believe I had gone to college to be a model. She thought it was a foolish move on my part— leaving a good-paying corporate position to pursue the unknown. My dad, on the other hand, responded with, "Whatever you want, baby." Don't misunderstand my mother. She admired my ambition and talent. She wanted me to be successful. It was just instinctual for her to try to protect me from the hurt she envisioned I would experience being among the big bad wolves. There were many days when I received letters of rejection. And there were days when I would meet with an agent face-to-face and I would be torn apart. But my mother was able to rest easier when I got my first acting gig within three months. And within seven months I got a consistent modeling gig—which lasted for the next decade!

As a model, I had the pleasure of working with Iman, Susan Lucci, Victoria Principal, Joan Rivers, Daphne Maxell Reid, and others. They are all wonderful people, which made the experience awesome. And soon, I was hosting a video show in New York City, the largest television market in the country. This gig gave me the opportunity to interview Queen Latifah, Shabba Ranks, Father MC, and others. But I still wanted my own talk show.

So, in 1996, I launched *S. Renee & Company* on the PAX Network in Philadelphia, Pennsylvania. I was very disappointed when it went off the air, as I had invested every dime I had and then some. My mind tried to use this perceived failure against my spirit, but my spirit wasn't having it. My mind would say, "See, I told you it wasn't going to work." But my spirit would stand up straight and tall and respond with, "But it served its purpose." My spirit had convinced my mind that some day I would become a national motivational speaker and a talk show host. When my mind began to back peddle, my spirit refused to budge. This gave me the strength to lick my wounds and persevere. I put together the best demo tape that I could and began my search for a hosting position in the country's fourth largest television market, Philadelphia.

As I went from interview to interview I would get the same response: you look good, sound great, but you need more experience. The interviewer would recommend that I go to a smaller market. I knew what God had spoken to my heart, so I would cancel every word that a person spoke that was contrary to what I knew was supposed to happen. And then I would reaffirm what was going to happen. I would say, "I cancel that in the name of Jesus. I'm going to host a show in Philadelphia." I would say it over and over again until I completely believed it!

Sounds crazy, right? But it's not. What you need to understand is the power of words and thoughts. Years ago I read a short, yet powerful book called *As a Man Thinketh* by James Allen. Once you read that book, you will never let anyone speak negative words to you again. Because you will understand the power of words and thoughts. You'll also become more mindful of your own thoughts. You don't have to use the phrase that I used. You can come up with your own affirmation. Because I bought into my affirmation, I didn't listen to anyone who told me I couldn't do it. However, every interview was a dead-end—until the day I turned on the television and saw the public affairs show that I was telling you about earlier—*Studio 57*. I became the host and producer of the show and the spokesperson for the station. I attended conferences, co-hosted telethons, hosted television specials, and served as a panelist for the New Jersey Gubernatorial Debates.

Are you uncertain about your future, your direction, and your purpose? Do you have big dreams inside of you that you don't know how to manifest? Here is some very simple advice: Ask For What You Want! Tell people what you need. Be honest about what you don't know and be open to advice. Once you make the decision to make destiny-directed decisions, you'll immediately face the naysayers. If you can overcome the first line of defense—which is usually yourself—over half the battle is won.

YOU CAN STILL HAVE PEACE OF MIND

Despite all the things we have to consider when making a decision, we shouldn't live life in fear. After every pep talk I gave myself about the importance of making good decisions, I felt empowered and ready to stand up against any temptation. I understood the basics, that I shouldn't smoke cigarettes, take drugs, drink alcohol, or succumb to peer pressure. I understood that education was important, and praying to God was a necessity.

Since I can remember, I would study and learn from other people's life lessons. When I saw hardship, I would wonder what happened, why it happened, and what choices the person made to get their particular result. I quickly realized that there are natural consequences to the decisions that we make. It became clear that some consequences can lead to what I call the "hole." This is the place where you experience feelings of guilt, uncertainty, anguish, abandonment, depression, and lack of control over your own life. You don't have to personally go in the "hole" to know that it's unpleasant. Just open your eyes and look around you.

Just open your ears and heart and listen to the experiences of others. I know what you're thinking: "But isn't life about learning lessons through my own experiences?" Yes, but it is often better—less painful, certainly—to learn lessons through other people's experiences. We don't have to take drugs to know they wreck our lives. We don't have to have a child to know that being a parent is financially and emotionally challenging. Yes, we're going to make mistakes, be impulsive, and use poor judgment at times. It's all part of becoming wiser. But we can minimize these errors if we listen to the people who love us. Our mothers, fathers, mentors, teachers, and friends can help to guide us around obstacles if we let them. They are trying to guide our lives to greatness. Like them, I can offer some tips that will assist you on your journey.

1. Know your values. Outline on paper what's important to you. Live according to your own standards and don't let anyone or anything change them—unless it will make you a better person.

2. Have a vision for your life and believe in it. Take ownership of this vision. Let it seep into the crevices of your soul until when you walk, it walks with you. When you talk, it talks. When you think, it produces your thoughts.

3. Listen to your gut. If it doesn't feel right, it isn't right. Don't rationalize against what you know you should or shouldn't do. Just listen to your gut and proceed accordingly.

4. Allow yourself the emotional and mental freedom to learn from wrong turns. Some things you just won't know until you get there. It's like the curve in the road. Learn the lesson and quickly move on. Don't let negative emotions guide your decisions. Honestly look within yourself and take responsibility for your role in the situation. Be sure your heart is pure as you move forward. This will ensure good judgment.

5. Ask questions, listen to and learn from wise souls. Especially those whom you know love you and have your best interests at heart. Ask yourself the following questions: "Which choice will move me toward my long range goals? What is the impact of this choice on those I love? Am I proud of this choice? If I make this choice, will I care if anyone knows I made it?"

6. Realize that you always have more than one choice. Every decision comes with options! Carefully examine all of your options before making a decision. If you can't clearly see more than one option, talk with someone you trust who can help you to see your options objectively.

7. When under pressure, don't be impulsive. Step back, look at the facts, and make a destiny-directed decision. At times, either option may lead to the same place, but you won't be in the same shape when you get there. If you give your options serious consideration before acting on your choice, you'll see that you can prevent a lot of heartache.

Continue building your personal assessment profile by responding to the following statements.

17. My personal philosophy on how I want to live my life in the following areas is...

Mentally:

_____

_____

Emotionally:

_____

_____

Physically:

_____

_____

Professionally:

_____

_____

Spiritually:

_____

_____

18. By living my values, I will gain...

_____

_____

19. Others around me will also benefit because...

_____

_____

20. I make a commitment to live my values by avoiding...

_____

_____

_____

_____

21. Fear will no longer stop me from...

_____

_____

_____

_____

22. I will make decisions that will move me toward...

_____

_____

_____

Chapter 4

TIME MANAGEMENT: IN THE INTEREST OF TIME

Procrastination is the number one killer of time.
And it has what I call "emotional feeders." These include fear of failing, fear of the
unknown, fear of embarrassment and boredom.

*O*ne day this thought hit me: "Time is the most important gift I have on earth." I began to think about all the wasted time and energy I had invested in activities and relationships—personal and professional—that weren't going anywhere. Time and energy I couldn't get back. My first thirty-some years of life were over. In an instant, I realized that I didn't know how much time I had left—and I needed to decide what I wanted to do with the remainder of my life.

I couldn't control the number of days I had left, but I could certainly plan how to most wisely spend them. One thing was clear: if I was committed to fulfilling my dreams, I needed to eliminate things, people, and situations that weren't helping me to grow and develop into the person that I saw in my vision. You also need to take inventory of your life. You have to ask yourself, "Is this going to serve me moving forward?" If yes, how? If no, let it go.

THE FIRST STEP TO SUCCESSFUL TIME MANAGEMENT IS CHANGE

When we're young, we think we have plenty of time. As we age, however, we think we don't have enough of it. So, it is critical to ask yourself, "How much time do I absolutely know I have?" The answer? That's right, only this moment.

We're not guaranteed the next second, and certainly not tomorrow. So, find your satisfaction, contentment, and impact in what is called the "now" moment. The "now" moment is living the precise moment you are experiencing. Have you ever been at school, but you were thinking about all the things you needed to do at work? How productive were you? Living in the now moment increases your quality of life and your effectiveness, regardless of what you are doing. Although we are a society that requires us to multi-task, the mind can only process one thought at a time. The body can only be in one place at a time. So, be there. Why stress yourself out?

You've probably heard many times before that the first step to making any change in your life is to acknowledge the need for change. Unfortunately, there have even been times when I've acknowledged the need for a change in my life, but nothing happened. That's because after I acknowledged the need for change, I continued doing the same things, in the same way, for the same reasons. Most people need a push to put them in motion. The desire is there, but they lack ambition. This is why it is critical that you know what motivates you to action. What has prompted you in the past to make a change? How crazy do you allow your life to get before you'll make a change? At what point do you say enough is enough? What do you need to make a change?

I believe that when a person recognizes a need for change, but either resists or ignores that need, they've buried their ambition beneath the issue that needs to be changed. So, they must elevate their ambition or desire. But how? By deliberately, intentionally, and strategically bringing about change. Change requires choice, commitment, focus, discipline, and intent. Let's look at choice first. What I've learned is that experiencing a state of craziness differs significantly from seeing yourself in a state of craziness. The truth is—in the visual, materialistic society in which we live—we have all learned to exist in a state of craziness, yet look sane. For example, couples appear to be happily married when they're in public, yet they can't communicate without yelling at one another when they're at home.

Make the choice to face yourself in silence and take responsibility for the state that you are in. Though your thoughts may scare you in the beginning, force yourself to stay and listen. You will find yourself trying to rationalize your craziness. This is an important process because your ambition will not rise above the issue until you understand the issue and can clearly see the benefit of changing.

After facing yourself and accepting the truth about who you are, and where you are in your life, make a commitment to change. Commitment means different things to different people. To ensure we are on the same page, let's agree that commitment means to see this process through until the end. So, you agree to the commitment of silencing any excuses and moving in the direction you've chosen until the new way of doing things becomes a habit. It helps to write down your commitment and post it in a visual place so that each day you can read and apply it to your life.

Personally, I had to overcome defending myself. I always felt personally attacked when a person would say anything that seemed like criticism. But after reading *The Four Agreements* by Don Miguel Ruiz, I realized that I was taking what people said too personally. So I wrote down my affirmations and posted them throughout my home that said, "I am okay as I am. I do not have to defend myself. I am a good listener. Change is good." After a while I found myself respecting and appreciating others for their opinion, regardless of whether or not I agreed with them.

Harness discipline and focus. These two qualities work hand in hand. In fact, you cannot have one without the other. You have to do what you commit to doing even when you don't feel like it. That's discipline. Being in the "now" moment takes focus. The best way to stay on track is to write down the personal benefit you will gain from the change. And finally, you have to have intent. This means that you will give the necessary attention to the specific areas of your life that you want to change. Whatever you anticipate to be the outcome, take the steps to get there. This includes taking responsibility for your actions—and everything that happens to you. Don't believe that your life is being taken away from you by some invisible force; you surrender it with your own doubts, fears, anxiety, and time wasting-tactics.

PROCRASTINATION: THE NUMBER ONE TIME-WASTING TACTIC

Most people have experienced feelings of anxiety and pressure when a five-page report is due the next day—and they have yet to pick out the subject. This is pure procrastination, the decision of putting something off until it's almost too late to start. Procrastination is a huge killer of time. It also has what I call "emotional feeders." These include fear of failing, fear of the unknown, fear of embarrassment when we have to depend on others for help, and boredom. These emotional feeders are fertile ground that enable procrastination to mushroom. But here are some things you can do to overcome it: First, write priorities every day, and then allocate time to complete each task. Put your least desirable tasks at a time of the day when you operate at peak performance. For some, this time may be in the morning and for others, later in the afternoon. If it is a large project that will consume a lot of time, set aside a few hours of uninterrupted time each day until the project is completed. Second, make a commitment to get started and set a date for completion. Be sure that the date is at least three to seven days in advance of your deadline. This will give you the breathing room you'll need to review it and make changes.

Good time management skills aren't difficult to learn. It's simple actually; just do what you know you should do and plan ahead. If getting to school or work on time requires you to get up earlier, then make the decision to set your alarm clock an hour ahead. Place it across the room, so that you're forced to get up and turn it off. If you notice that you are constantly late getting to a particular place, check to see if you're giving it enough priority. Review your goals and decide what is important to you. A lack of priorities leads to mismanaged time. Here are some tips on dealing with time wasters.

1. Avoid gossip sessions: Gossip sessions are huge time wasters and energy robbers. And gossip is neither healthy nor helpful for you. Delete it from your life.

2. Use time between meetings, appointments, and classes: Always have something enjoyable to read or work on. It is unprofessional for individuals to be late for a scheduled appointment or meeting. But if you're kept waiting, this is an ideal time to catch up on some missed reading. So bring a magazine with you. Or develop your "To Do" list. Just make sure you're doing something productive. This will keep your mind off the person being late, and your body and mind calm. I keep at least one book in my car in case there's a traffic jam or accident. This also keeps me calm and feeling productive. Just don't read while driving!

3. Guard your shoulder: Being a supportive listener is a wonderful way to show your love for others. There are times, however, when it is clear that the person crying on your shoulder isn't ready to make a change in his or her life and are infringing on your time. Gently tell the person you would be happy to get back with them when you have a free moment.

4. Draw the line on hold calls: When you hear that familiar beep during a phone conversation with a friend, and she asks you to hold on a second while she takes the incoming call, don't wait on the line for more than 20 seconds. Hang up! If it is you who needs to take the second caller, politely end the first call. Otherwise, let them leave a message.

5. Don't worry and whine about things you can't control: Until you understand that, you will never truly be free. Ninety percent of what you worry about will not happen. So, what are you worried about? If the situation is something you can't control, like another person's behavior, the weather, or something that has happened in the past, simply let it go.

6. Keep your agenda first: Everything is urgent to the person needing it. If someone wants something done that will put you under pressure and in a bind, tell them that you are committed to another project and that you can't help them. And don't feel guilty. You don't owe anyone your time. It is a gift from you to them and vice-versa. Remember that everyone has an agenda and will make their agenda your priorities. So ask yourself daily, "What is my agenda?"

Take a moment to think about and complete the following statements.

23. My greatest asset is...

_____

24. The amount of time I have left is...

_____

25. For the rest of my life I would like to spend my time...

_____

_____

_____

26. I typically realize that it's time for a change when...

_____

_____

_____

27. I spend my time...

_____

_____

_____

28. The least productive things that I do or worry about that causes me to lose a lot of time are...

_____

_____

29. I would be happier and more productive if I eliminated the following people, things, and situations from my life...

_____

_____

_____

30. The emotional feeders to my procrastination are...

_____

_____

_____

31. Because I feed my procrastination and wait until the last minute to complete tasks, I'm causing myself...

_____

_____

_____

32. I don't like to feel stressed and overwhelmed so I commit to myself to...

_____

_____

_____

33. The people, things, and situations that are most important to me are...

_____

_____

_____

34. My day will be determined by my priorities. This is the beginning of my ongoing list.

The projects that need my immediate attention are...

_____ To Be Completed On____/____/____

_____To Be Completed On____/____/____

_____To Be Completed On____/____/____

_____To Be Completed On____/____/____

_____To Be Completed On____/____/____

_____To Be Completed On____/____/____

_____To Be Completed On____/____/____

_____To Be Completed On____/____/____

_____To Be Completed On____/____/____

35. The personal benefits I will gain from changing are...

_____

_____

_____

Chapter 5

ATTITUDE:
YOUR REPRESENTATIVE

Say it until you believe it.
Say it until it becomes part of you.
Say it until it is you.

Everyone has an attitude about life. Some people are so positive that you can't wait to be around them. Some people are so negative it's hard to be around them. Even before a person speaks, you can see it in their walk and feel it in their presence. Our attitudes create an invisible, yet unmistakable energy force. Some call it "aura." Others refer to it as "spirit." Still others refer to it as "vibe." Regardless of what you call it, this energy force represents you—and acts as your calling card to the world.

A positive attitude is the most powerful tool you can develop, which will help you get through life more successfully. It helps you to see the good in a bad situation. It creates hope in the midst of hopelessness. It helps to lessen the sting of pain. It creates career opportunities. It saves broken marriages and relationships. It creates an extraordinary life for its owner.

At the core of who we are is our attitude, which makes up our belief system, our mannerisms, our behavior, and our thoughts and feelings. The greatest thing about our attitude is that we can choose to change it at will. Whenever we decide that we don't like the "vibes" that we are sending, we can change it. We're that powerful! Our outlook, behavior, mannerisms, thoughts, feelings, and world can change significantly just by our choosing to change our attitude.

Do you doubt this? Then read the biography of any great leader or successful person and you'll see that they have a positive, enthusiastic attitude. Eighty-five percent of success is attitude, while 15 percent comes from skills and knowledge. And yet 95 percent of all corporate training focuses on knowledge! That's why companies are desperate to hire people with the "right attitude." A recruiter told me that his company looks for people with people skills and a positive attitude because they can teach employees the how to's of the business.

DO YOU HAVE THE RIGHT STUFF?

Self-assessment can be a challenge for most people because no one wants to admit that they have "baggage." We are creatures of habit. We resist change. Successful people, however, know the importance of looking at themselves and surrendering to change. If you want to "live a good life," then understand that you have to create it. And your attitude is the starting point.

The first step to creating a positive attitude is to take note of yourself. Do you feel comfortable around people who are positive? When unpleasant situations arise, do you expect good to come of it? Do you expect people to like you? Are you friends with people who are focused, motivated, and doing the right thing? Do you expect great things from yourself? Are you prepared to work for what you want out of life? Are you cooperative when things don't go your way? Do you frequently use words like "please" and "thank you"? Do you listen to people who are trying to help you? Can you quickly diffuse conflict? Are you friendly? Do opportunities frequently present themselves to you? If you answered yes to the majority of these questions, more than likely you are a positive person and you successfully convey that message to others.

However, if you frequently find yourself in conflict with others, are continuously defending your behavior, judging others who are confident and positive, avoiding people who are doing well for themselves, constantly talking about how bad things are, selling yourself short, and seldom display a friendly demeanor, then you are cheating yourself. If you change your attitude, you will totally change your life!

Some ways to change your attitude is by reading self-help books, listening to motivational tapes, and surrounding yourself with positive people. But you must stay with it. Studies show that if you hear something today, you will maintain only 50 percent of it over the next twenty-four hours, 25 percent over the next forty-eight hours, and only 2 percent over the next sixteen days. In order to maintain and be able to use information, you have to hear it over and over again.

Do you know why it is so easy, on the other hand, to retain negative information? By the age of five, 77 percent of the messages we received were negative. We heard our parents, teachers, and those in authority; say "no" more than "yes." We were warned of the dangers more than told of the rewards when we attempted new challenges. We unconsciously owned these messages, which became our thoughts and molded our lives. Once we begin to face challenges and realize that we don't have the courage and stamina to overcome the obstacles, that's when we understand the need to reverse the ill effects of our upbringing. You don't have to wait until that moment comes to make a change. Start today.

You begin by changing how you think. I've been into personal development since my early teens and I continue to read, listen to tapes, and expose myself to people that I can feed off of and who can feed off of me. And I'm still learning. I'm not scared to say, "I don't know." I can say, "Will you help me?" and not feel weak. My attitude about life, living, and myself gets better every day because of what I feed my mind.

Superior power and performance comes from what you feed your mind. Whatever goes in, comes out. This includes the music you listen to, the images you expose yourself to, and the people and the words that you invite into your world. Protect your mind! Every word that is spoken to you, every lyric that you hear, and every image that you see, shapes your attitude. America is the land of the free. You can find some of the raunchiest, vulgar music and images in America. But you can also find some of the most inspirational, breathtaking music and images in America. You can expose yourself to whatever you choose. It is all in what you're looking for. What you're looking for really comes down to the answers to these four questions: "Who am I?" "How do I really feel about myself?" "How do I want to live my life?" and "What do I want to give and get out of my life?"

Once you honestly answer these questions and understand that you alone decide how you want to think, you are on your way to the life that I believe you're hoping for. It works like this: What you see, hear, and experience creates thoughts; thoughts create actions; actions create opportunities; and people who are prepared for the opportunities create results.

The key is implementation. Write down whatever you want to accomplish, and hang your goals in your bedroom, bathroom, kitchen, car, etc. Just seeing them every day will motivate you to act on them.

Write down positive, life-changing affirmations and say them aloud every day. Affirmations are statements that you declare as truth. For example, if you're working on your self-esteem, say something like: "I am confident. I love myself. I respect myself and others. I am unique and special." Once you have them written down, say it until you believe it. Say it until it becomes a part of you. Say it until it *is* you. Words have such life, energy, and force in them that things will begin to happen in your life that you won't be able to explain!

CHANGE IS GOOD

Here are some tips that will empower you as you transition into the person you want to become.

1. Have a genuine interest in others. Motivational guru Zig Ziglar once said, "People don't care how much you know, until they know how much you care about *them*." Life is a cycle of giving, getting, learning, and teaching. Regardless of what you decide to become in life, be sensitive to the needs and feelings of others. That doesn't mean that you lower your standards to someone else's. It means only that you try to build a bridge with and to others by truly caring about them.

2. Learn to listen. Communication is dialogue-not a monologue. Have you ever met people who monopolize the conversation? What did you do the next time you saw them? You tried to avoid them, right? Having excellent communication skills includes listening. This is especially true in social situations. Find ways to get others talking. You will be amazed at how interesting others are when you begin to care enough about them to listen to what they are saying.

3. Don't boast. There is a fine line between sharing a success story and boasting. It's best to allow others to bring up your achievements, and if asked about them, make it brief and concise.

4. Be personable. Be pleasant in your presentation and personality. This has a lot to do with your style of dress, mannerisms, and communication skills. Unfortunately, we all have our stereotypes and prejudices. These stereotypes aren't just based on race, age, religion, education, or social status. It's how you dress, walk, talk, and interact with others. The way you dress is your personal preference, but it will determine how you're perceived in society. It's called image. Image is all around us. We can't escape its hold on us or our society. It always has been and, I suspect, always will be a tremendous part of who we are.

Just as you don't buy just anything, don't present yourself as just anything. When you buy a product, you're buying the perception or image of the product. You are buying what has been strategically presented to you as something that will make your life better—that if you use it you'll be more beautiful, sexier, healthier, or smarter.

Companies spend millions of dollars developing and protecting their image. They spend millions more studying the way we dress, act, think, and buy. Some marketing researchers undoubtedly know more about our preferences than we do ourselves!

As the media exposes more problems with products, employee concerns, and business integrity issues, image preservation has become a priority. You don't have to spend millions developing and preserving your image, but you should carefully design and protect your image. Your image will determine your income, the type of person who is attracted to you, and the level of respect that you receive. This is going to increase your confidence and the impact you make on others. When people decide to let you into their lives, either personally or professionally, it's often based on their perception of you. If you can't leave in their minds a strong perception that you have the right character, attitude, and skills, you're going miss out on many great opportunities.

I was speaking to a public relations class at a university and I was amazed at the students' appearance. It was obvious from the questions that they asked that they were intelligent. But some of the students had tattoos and earrings in their noses and tongues. And some sported blue and green hair and wool hats in the classroom. In a friendly, sensitive manner, I addressed my concern about their appearance. One of the students talked about being unique and wanting to be respected for her uniqueness. I posed a question to her. I said, "If you became seriously ill and went to the emergency room, and found yourself in the examining room with a doctor with long blue hair and earrings in his nose and tongue, what would you say?" She said, "I would say, 'You are not my doctor.'" I replied, "That's exactly what an interviewer is going to say to you. The interviewer may not be so direct, but you won't get the job."

Some young people use the popular saying, "I'm keepin' it real" to justify their negative behavior and slouchy presentation. They don't realize that their circumstances, or the environment in which they were raised is not who they are. Of course, it has influenced their life, but their greatness is locked within them and they create their own reality. What is real about marking your body with fads like belly rings and tattoos? Blue hair and baggy pants, whose reality is that?

How you walk, sit, stand, and stoop all create a mental picture of your attitude about life. Do you maintain good posture, which communicates that you're alert, confident, and able? Or does your posture say, "I don't feel good about myself; I'm boring and lazy." What about your facial expression? Is it pleasant, natural, at ease, and welcoming? Or does it communicate that you're tense, unhappy, stressed, and irritated? Fifty-five percent of communication is facial expression, which accurately reflects your thoughts. Thirty-eight percent of communication is verbal, and 7 percent are the words you choose to use. How are your verbal skills? Are you concise and to the point when expressing yourself? Are you articulate? Or is your vocabulary so weak that you have to depend on slang and profanity to get you through? Record yourself cussing and cursing. Regardless of how articulate you are, you'll most likely note how horrible it sounds.

Your ability to develop yourself into a package of excellent communication skills, with superior presence and a dynamic attitude, will take you places that you never thought you could go. And just the opposite is true: If you fail to develop these skills, you will limit yourself. The number one complaint of employers is that potential hires can't communicate.

People buy from people they like and trust. If you never give them a chance to get to know you, because of your image, then you will shortchange yourself. What image are you projecting? Be honest. When you look in the mirror, would you trust the person staring back at you?

Now that you know this, be realistic about your employment, and personal and professional relationship opportunities. You can be smart, friendly, and personable, but your physical presentation completes the package.

5. Celebrate diversity. Every person has merit. I know that I just spent time talking about the impact of image and what I'm about to say doesn't change that. It is, however, important to give people a chance and to celebrate them as individuals, regardless of color, educational background, social status, religion, age, and size.

In social situations, I notice that people segregate themselves. It has been proven that people are more comfortable with people who look like them, but it has also been proven that there is tremendous power, insight, and creativity in diversity. Because I believe in the power of diversity, I try to keep an open mind in all situations.

In social situations, I make it a point to meet someone who is different from me. I've met some amazing people employing this method. I especially like going to tables where people are different from me. Yes, it can be intimidating, but I simply walk over and say, "Hi! Is anyone sitting here?" It seems like time stops as they all look at me in a daze. I then hear, "Oh no, help yourself." I do this because I think it is important to send the message that I'm comfortable with you and myself—regardless of our differences—and that I don't have to only be around people who look like me to feel secure. If you get to know me and I get to know you, our lives will be enriched because of our time together. Sometimes I'm received with friendly, open arms and sometimes I'm not. And that's okay.

LET YOUR POSITIVE ATTITUDE OVERSHADOW ADVERSITY

A part of life is facing various challenges. A part of those challenges will include times when people upset you and you upset them. There will be times when situations don't go your way. That's life. How you handle yourself during these times is going to expose you to yourself. Do you get frustrated? Do you have feelings of rage inside? Or do you see the challenge for what it is, an opportunity to see yourself maintain peace and use good judgment?

This is what I would recommend. Have a presence of readiness and can do. When you know yourself, your talents, your power, and your unlimited capacity to make things happen in your life, you can begin to project a presence of readiness and can-do. It looks and sounds like this: Your posture is erect, but not stiff. You are alert and experiencing the now moment. You are listening to and in tune with the people and situations around you. You have a warm, welcoming smile. Your handshake is firm. Your eyes say, "I'm capable and here to contribute." You acknowledge the presence and significance of everyone. You speak when you know that you have something significant to say. Your comments celebrate others and burst with wisdom and positiveness.

Here are some answers to concerns you might have:

1. I don't know where to begin. Start where you are. Forget the past and begin a new journey today. Start fresh every morning. If you are angry with someone, forgive them. If their actions do not meet your expectations, let it go. You make mistakes, I make mistakes, everybody makes mistakes. Don't dwell on it.

2. I don't have time. If you say you don't have time, you're right. We always believe ourselves. Remember time management is about priorities. Make developing yourself into a better person your highest priority. I promise, it will be worth the investment.

3. I feel intimidated and I don't know how to act around certain people. Just be genuine. Most people will willingly accept you into their circle. Having a mentor will help. Just be open and ready to learn. People who are positive and enjoy helping people understand that you are new to this process. Every teacher wants a willing student. And every student wants a willing teacher. Both of your needs will be met.

4. How will I know if the principles are working? You'll notice a change in yourself as you deal with situations. You'll see yourself growing before your very eyes. You'll feel it and others will, too. People will be drawn to you. They will comment about your presence, personality, aura or spirit. I assure you, a consistent change—positive or negative—doesn't go unnoticed. Just keep in mind that you're going to make mistakes along the way, but keep trying. You didn't develop the habits you have overnight, so don't expect them to magically disappear. It takes work! In the end you'll see that the satisfaction is so much greater than the effort.

Complete the following statements.

36. When I'm around confident, positive people I feel...

_____

_____

_____

37. Most of my friends are (focused, motivated, drinkers, lazy, etc.)...

_____

_____

_____

38. When things go wrong I typically...

_____

_____

_____

39. When I interact with people, my attitude says that I'm...

_____

_____

_____

40. My attitude is consistently...

_____

_____

41. The following are characteristics that I would change about my attitude and why...

_____

_____

42. I currently feed my mind oral and visual information that says...

_____

_____

43. I can help myself by feeding my mind information about...

_____

_____

44. To create a new attitude and a better life for myself, I commit to doing the following for the next thirty days...

_____

_____

_____

_____

45. My three affirmations for the next thirty days are...

_____

_____

_____

46. My current image would be described as...

_____

_____

_____

47. I prefer to present an image of...

_____

_____

_____

48. I will change the following to improve my image...

_____

_____

_____

_____

_____

_____

49. Once I make the necessary changes I expect...

_____

_____

_____

_____

Chapter 6

NEW PERSPECTIVE:
DON'T CHANGE WHO YOU ARE,
JUST CHANGE THE WAY YOU THINK

You can't choose how you're going to die, so choose how you're going to live.

Now it's time to pull it all together and make it work for you. In Chapter One, Human Uniqueness: Preparing for the Fight, I shared information that I hope helped you to find and protect your internal uniqueness. Use this chapter as a constant reminder that life is simply a compilation of many events. Every event has a purpose, which is to bring shape to your uniqueness so that others will be blessed by your presence. In Chapter Two, Self-Image: You Have the Power, I desperately wanted you to learn how to trust yourself, build your self-esteem, and overcome obstacles that can derail you from your divine purpose. Live by the principles and you'll find that no matter how many times you fall, you'll always find the strength to get up again. In Chapter Three, Decision Making: It's All Up to You, my deepest desire is to have shared wisdom that will serve you a lifetime. As you make decisions that are shaping your life, I trust that courage, integrity, hard work, perseverance, and passion steer you in the right direction. While you are moving in the right direction, I know that the skills that you will develop from the information shared in Chapter Four, Time Management: In the Interest of

Time, will serve you well. Learning to let go of the emotional feeders that hinder your success will be liberating. And in Chapter Five, Attitude: Your Representative, I included the importance of having a polished public image, superior communication skills, a sincere interest in others, and developing and maintaining the right attitude about life because these are essential to "making it in life." Now it is time to understand why and how to make it work for you.

YOUR OPTIONS ARE IN LIFE

It may seem a bit unusual to talk about death in a self-help book, but I see death as a part of life, one of the many events that you and I will experience. As I witnessed death render my grandmother physically powerless, I realized that our options are in life. My grandmother lived seventy-six years and she crossed over within two months of discovering she had cancer. The most important lesson I learned while watching her body shut down, is that death is only one the many events that we experience in life. It is our final transition. How we live has far greater impact than how and when we die. Have you ever asked yourself, "What would this world be like without me?" What about the question: "What is it about me that would be missed if I were to cross over today?"

In the space that we travel, we leave an impression on everyone we meet. Whenever two or more people get together and your name comes up, they share their impressions of you with one another. What is your story? How is it told?

YOU NEED A PLAN

With or without a plan, we're not going to live each day perfectly. We're growing and learning each day. Like I've said, it's a process. As I work my plan to achieve my goals, I trust God to honor my efforts. Do I get off-course despite my plan? Sometimes, it seems so. I believe, however, that everything works for my good and according to God's master plan. When I lay out my plan, I don't know all the details—the people I need to meet and things I need to experience for my plan to work. That's where faith comes in. You have to have faith in yourself and believe that, in the end, things work out for the best. Does having faith mean that you won't have challenges? No. In fact, when you have a challenge and you want to overcome it, you have to apply your faith. What is faith? Faith is knowing that the invisible exists—your feelings, thoughts, intuitions, and beliefs—and they create the tangible. Your faith has to give you the strength to trust that what you desire and need will be granted. That doesn't mean that it's going to be granted exactly how you want it. Remember, your life experiences will unfold according to the big picture!

Because we create whatever is in our lives, it's important that we use our time and talents wisely. Are you wondering where to start? An older and wiser friend explained it to me this way: start where you are, use what you have, and do the best you can.

I have three questions for you: Do you know the difference between what is real or imagined? How real are your thoughts, dreams, and visions? Can they really come true?

Samuel Taylor Coleridge asks it like this:

What if you slept?
And what if, in your sleep you dreamed?
And what if, in your dream you went to heaven
and there plucked a strange and beautiful flower?
And what if, when you awoke, you had the flower in your hand?

The truth is, you decide what is real or imagined. Your choice will determine your actions. If you find that place of knowing in your life, it will take you to places that you thought you were only imagining you could go. My mother says, "I know that I know that I know." And what is it that she knows? Only she knows! And in her world only she needs to know. Others don't have to believe in what you "know" in order for your dreams to come true. The power is inside of you.

Once you decide what is real, develop a plan around *your* reality. Build your life around the reality you have decided to create. If you work and make decisions according to the control that you now realize you have over your life, you will be less likely to get sidetracked by individuals who think they know you better than you know yourself. I decided a long time ago that I wasn't giving anyone my permission to define me. Not my friends, not my teachers, not the media.

We often empower undeserving people by allowing them to tell us who we are and how far we can go. We put our faith and trust in them. The truth is, what do they know about us and what God has for us? Set your own standards and watch others respect and follow you. You will eventually develop a confidence that says, "I know who I am, I know where I'm going, and I'm excited to be on the right path." Stay focused. Be consistent in who you are and just watch your reputation of respect build.

I can recall when I first understood this profound lesson. When I was growing up there were two middle schools. They both taught fifth through eighth grades. I attended fifth and half of sixth grade at Central Middle. There I was teased, picked on, my lunch money was taken, and I was constantly threatened by the bullies. I was terrified. The only thing I could think about was how I could fit in. What did I need to do to fit in? How could I win these people over? Their reign of terror came to an end when I moved to a new neighborhood, which required me to attend William Henry Middle School.

As with most people, I was concerned about being accepted and liked. I wondered if the kids would harass me as they did at the old school. But I decided that that wasn't going to happen. This was a new start for me and I was going to build my reputation differently. I wasn't going to be the timid, "I don't know what I want, you can take advantage of me" person anymore. But when I got there, it was more than a notion. Of course, there was the bully and her entourage waiting to put fear in my heart. What was I going to do? I wasn't a fighter. In fact, I feared fighting even when I wasn't the one fighting. But this was my moment. I had to dig deep and find the courage to be me. This meant that I had to do what I most feared doing—stand up for myself and make my position known. Not only to them, but to myself.

The group of girls invited me to join their group. But I didn't want to, because I understood the consequences of being part of such a group. It meant that there was one leader and everyone else were followers. If one leader didn't like someone, the rest of the group didn't either. Being in this group meant that someone else would dictate how I should feel and act toward others. That wasn't me. Those days were over! I wanted to be me. I wanted to be friends with everyone. I tried to get these girls to understand, but they turned on me. They started by trying to intimidate me with the "I don't like you" stuff. It didn't work. So, they decided that they were going to beat me up! We were in gym class and each girl took her turn hitting me in the back of the head as she ran by. I sat quietly and watched the girls as they laughed and joked at me. Little did they know that I was looking for the weakest link. I found her. When she ran by and hit me, I got up and ran after her. I threw a few punches…thank God it didn't last long. Before I knew it, I was in the guidance counselor's office. No one could understand why "the good girl was fighting." After that incident, I never had to worry about being intimidated by my classmates again. I did exactly what I said I was going to do. I became friends with everyone. I was a leader. I was consistent, respectful, and fair to everyone. I showed that I was a leader. And my classmates honored that. In fact, two years later the student body voted me Queen and most popular, best dressed, friendliest, and most reliable!

Establishing and expecting more for yourself is so contagious that even you'll begin to wonder why you're so popular. In general, people want what is good. The problem is that they just don't have the nerve, the fight, or the discipline to get it. It is lonely at times. You have to decide if you want to settle at being just average. But if you decide that you want more, and that you're ready to stand alone if necessary to get it, here are a few tips for your journey:

1. Always be positive. Be thankful for the good. Whenever things look bleak, still look for the good. Don't be drawn into negative talk about others. Be upbeat in your walk. Walk like you have a purpose. Walk like you have somewhere to go and it's important that you get there, even if you're just going to class. Your walk speaks volumes about you.

2. Be friendly to everyone. This includes those who are considered outcasts. They may not look like you or act the way you think they should, but all people are human beings. They have feelings. Just like you, they want to be accepted, complimented, and encouraged. They want someone to care about them.

Smile not only with your lips, but with your voice. Look others directly in the eye. Be genuine as you interact with people. People typically respond in kind. If you're friendly to them, they'll be friendly to you. If they aren't, something is probably on their mind. Maybe even troubling them. Even though they don't respond immediately, your friendliness could be their symbol of hope for a better day. You would be amazed by what a smile can do for someone.

This method of interacting with people really works. It is what got me the accolades in eighth grade and during my senior year of high school, where I was voted friendliest and best personality. People are drawn to people who are positive and sensitive to the "now" moment and their state of mind. Here's an example. Recently, my nephew and I were in a retail store and the cashier didn't speak nor did she acknowledge our presence. I asked her, "Is this a nice place to work? You don't seem happy." She looked at me, smiled and said, "Oh, I just had the two worst customers. I can't believe people can be so mean and it isn't even 6 a.m. yet." She looked directly into my eyes. I smiled at her and she said, "But it's going to get better from here. The sun is beginning to come out. It's going to be a beautiful day." I smiled and responded, "Absolutely." Notice that I didn't do anything but ask a question based on what was happening in the moment. That technique is what I call "Shifting the Energy."

Shifting the Energy requires you to be in and acknowledge what is happening in the present moment. It is easy to do and the results are amazing. Acknowledging someone's negative behavior with a question or a smile raises their awareness of their present state of mind. We exist either in a conscious or unconscious state. We continually experience a range of emotions in our conscious and unconscious mind. At times, we are so unaware and disconnected from our conscious state that we don't even realize the non-verbal message (energy) that we send to others. When you are connected and living in the present moment, you can shift energy at will.

3. Have a plan. Of all the people I've talked to, I've never heard anyone say they want to live life on the street, on the run, or be dependent on others. None of them said they wanted to be a prostitute, drug addict, stripper, or pimp. I know that you have big dreams in your heart. Your dreams can come true if you set goals, develop a plan, and make decisions that lead you to where you want to go. Studies show that people who set goals on a regular basis are in the top 3 percent of the population that is considered "successful." You should also research how others in the same position got to where you want to go. If you follow your written plan, it will give you unbelievable focus and purpose. It will transform the way you navigate through life. Each day you will be a step closer to your dream.

Before long, you'll be able to see it and hear it. When you're faced with a challenge, the small stuff won't seem like a mountain. Your view of life will change. Your plan will even guide your decisions. You'll realize that what you perceived as impossibilities are really possible.

Let me share another eighth grade experience with you. My school used tests to identify the "smartest" students—and the "dumbest" students. Group One was the top and Group Four was at the bottom. I was put in Group Two. But I wasn't happy that someone else decided that I wasn't smart enough to function at the highest level possible. So I marched down to the office of one of the school's guidance counselors. I shared my concerns with him and he gave me permission to take on the challenge of moving up to Group One. He made it clear, however, that if I was unsuccessful during the first marking period, I would be reassigned to Group Two. Was I successful? Depends on what you define as success. According to my standard of success at the time, I was successful. I wasn't an A student. In fact, my grades reflected the fact that I was definitely being challenged. Most people would probably say that I was in over my head. And there were times that I would have agreed that I had bitten off more than I could chew. But I kept trying. I passed the eighth grade.

That year, I was the only recipient of the John W. Taylor award. This award represented my commitment to embrace challenge. It was the highest award given to an eighth grader. My guidance counselor believed in me, and that belief allowed me to believe more in myself. But the belief originated in me. I sold him on the possibility. He bought into it. And when it seemed like I couldn't handle the work he didn't panic. His faith remained steady. In return I didn't give up on myself. I simply did my best and that was enough for him and me.

Most important, I proved to myself that even when people in authority put a label on me, I don't have to accept the label as truth. And a test certainly couldn't measure my determination and willingness to work hard for what I wanted. I was prepared to invest the necessary time and energy to live up to my own expectations. And yes, I expected great things of myself. That was the key in this situation. My determination and belief in myself were of greater value than my grades. If it were based solely on grades, I should have stayed in Group Two because I probably would have earned higher grades. And being moved to Group Three wouldn't have been totally out of the question. Sometimes it's not about the result as much as the process. Of greater significance, it's about your understanding of what you want to get out of the experience.

If you want respect, be prepared to earn it. Don't stand on top of the mountain and beat your chest yelling, "Give me respect!" without having the desire and ambition to prove your worthiness to receive it. People won't give respect until it is earned. So, start now. It doesn't matter where you go, your reputation will precede you.

WHY HAVE A PLAN?

Everyone has a story to tell about how proud and exciting it feels to achieve a goal. Whether it's receiving recognition for being the top salesperson of the month, being acknowledged for completing a task successfully at work, standing up to the school bully, or being elected student government president—success feels good! I can't tell you the numerous things I've been blessed to accomplish because I was in the right place, with the right skills, at the right time, doing the right thing. But as I look back over my life, I realize I had many missed opportunities because I didn't have a carefully laid out plan.

For example, in 1984 and again in 1985, I ran for Youth of the Year for the First Episcopal District of the African Methodist Episcopal (AME) Church. Did I set out to become Youth of the Year? No, I didn't. In fact, someone approached me about competing, so I did.

Winning the title didn't become important until the day I looked my competitors in the eye, wished them well, and secretly said to myself, "Bring it on." When I felt the adrenaline flowing through my body as the moderator began the countdown to the timed test. When while on stage I felt the energy of the audience enjoying my presentation through their applause and laughter. When the announcer declared me the second place winner, it was at that moment—as I watched the winner gleam with excitement and heard the thunder of applause from the audience—that *I* wanted to be the winner. I invested many hours preparing for each competition. Many people devoted an immeasurable amount of time helping me to prepare for the competitive events within the contest. Unfortunately, I failed to see that studying, traveling, and preparing for the competitions were steps toward winning. In my mind, I didn't connect them to the desired result. And no one explained to me the process. So how could it have been a victory when I didn't purpose within myself to be victorious?

The competition was based on the contestants' knowledge of the history and process of the AME Church, a talent presentation, and their school, community, and church activities. Each contestant first competed in their home district. The winner of each district then moved to the conference level. The first year I won the district competition, but lost the conference contest. The second year, I won the conference title. That year I went on to compete against the top six other extremely talented youth from Philadelphia, New England, New Jersey, Bermuda, New York and Western New York Conferences. The youth were well prepared, well rehearsed, and ready to win.

The most difficult lesson I had to learn in receiving second place honors was the difference in expecting to win and planning to win. As a part of the final competition, each contestant had to identify a person to introduce them during the talent segment of the competition. The judges evaluated you on the introduction and your performance. All contestants were asked, in advance, to identify a person of their choice to introduce them. Well, I forgot. Why? Because I expected to win, but didn't plan to win. So, just before the talent segment was about to begin, one of the intermediaries asked me, "Who is going to introduce you?" Dumbfounded, I began my quest to identify someone. With little time to spare, I grabbed someone (I don't even remember who) and gave her a few things to say and decided to "let the chips fall where they may." And that's exactly where they fell.

Later, I was told that the competition was so close. This was a moment when I had to admit that God had given me everything that I needed to win—and I had dropped the ball. Put simply, without a plan I forgot to do what needed to be done to win. Was winning the contest that important? No. But the fact that I could have won and didn't because I failed to plan was. Back then I was totally responsible for my success. Today, I am totally responsible for my success. Likewise, you are totally responsible for your success. Will obstacles come? Yeah. Will you have moments of uncertainty and feelings of being overwhelmed? Yeah. Will you sometimes feel like giving up? Yeah. Will you wonder if it's worth it? Absolutely!

When you're feeling discouraged and uncertain about life, you'll look at your plan and know that you have a purpose. You'll look at your list of God-given talents and be grateful. You'll review all that you've accomplished and be inspired. You'll look at your goals and be motivated. A plan will give you the hope you need to achieve your purpose and live your vision.

The choice is yours. You can go through life giving your best, but not understanding why you're giving your best or what the results of your hard work should be. Or you can have a plan that gives you focus, confidence, and endurance to know that the possibilities are truly possible. For every successful mission in this world there's a strategic, written plan. When a couple builds a house, there's a plan. When a company develops and markets a new product, there's a plan. When a family decides to take a trip, there's a plan. Why would you attempt to travel life's journey without a plan?

MAKE THE PRINCIPLES WORK FOR YOU

In 2003, I attended the National Football League Hall of Fame Fortieth Anniversary Festival. The event was awesome. To be in an atmosphere where the best football players in this country were celebrated for breaking records and surpassing personal and professional goals was extremely inspiring. Each of these legends gave their advice to young people yearning to be great at something. Elvin Bethea, the oldest of the group, described his journey as one requiring self-discipline, focus, inner drive, and a strong work ethic. He quoted a former coach as saying, "You practice like you play." With that in mind, he always gave 100 percent the moment he stepped onto the practice field. His Hall of Fame honor was the result of his hard work and dedication. Marcus Allen, the youngest of the group, said playing football and earning top honors was what he lived for. He set the goal, held onto his dream, and refused to be persuaded by friends to abandon his dream. He purposed in his heart to be the best. His success came from his commitment to his ideas and values. James Lofton spoke of having passion and said that no matter what you decide to do, you have to love what you do. And Joe DeLamielleure spoke of the importance of having fun at doing whatever you decide to do.

Clearly, it takes courage to live a life of high standards. Every great leader faces ridicule and controversy, especially when they don't follow the crowd or conform to society's expectations. I know that you want be strong and do well. And you can be strong and do well. Just make the decision to do so. Not for anyone else, but for yourself.

Being angry, deceptive, and defiant doesn't hurt anyone but you. Yes, it causes pain to the ones who love you, but it hurts you more—

spiritually, mentally, emotionally, and physically. I'm always saddened when I meet adult men and women who are unhappy or discontent. My heart goes out to adults who are embarrassed and ashamed. They live in darkness, guilt, and self-pity because they let opportunities get away. They are scared children in adult bodies. Don't let that happen to you.

Take a moment and close your eyes. Think about all the learning, jobs, community service, and relationship-building opportunities that you have let slip away from you. Go ahead, close your eyes. Do you see that you have to make plans to be successful? If you now realize that you have let one too many opportunities pass you by, don't live life in remorse. Just seize the next opportunity...and the next one. Open yourself up to the possibilities. Take some tips from people you admire and trust and create your own "good life." Here are a few of my own tips:

1. Take pride in yourself and your work. Don't rush to get things done, just because you want to say that they're done. Take pride in what you do. Give it all you've got at that moment. As NFL Hall of Fame inductee Elvin Bethea did, practice like you play. Fix yourself up. Wear your clothes; don't let your clothes wear you.

2. Don't stop trying. Keep pushing. Some of the greatest athletes made their coaches wonder what they were thinking when they recruited them. Don't give up. It gets better and easier. The more you give of yourself, the more you see in yourself. When you've given what you believe to be all you have, keep trying. You'll surprise yourself. *There Is More Inside.*

3. Watch how you spend. I'm not a financial advisor, but I wish I had sought one out earlier in my life. Perhaps as early as after my high school graduation. Connect with people who can help you set up a budget and save according to your future financial plans. Search until you find someone you trust. And use that intuitive gut thing that I talked about earlier! For starters consider reading *"7 Money Mantras For A Richer Life: How to Live Well with the Money You Have,"* by Financial Columnist Michelle Singletary. If you start now, you'll at least begin to understand the impact finances have on your life.

4. Network, Network, Network. I heard this term all the time in college, but no one explained what it meant or how to do it. I didn't understand the power of networking until a friend explained to me a concept called "Six Degrees of Separation." It was explained to me this way: Any person that you meet is within six people of a person that you need to meet. The person that you know or the person that they know can make one call and start the ball rolling toward a job or contract. Remember, people like to work with and buy from people they know and trust. So, attend events and make yourself known. The following networking tips from the experts will help you.

a. Firmly shake a person's hand and look them in the eyes.

b. Listen and always bring the conversation back to the other person.

c. Have a 30-second speech that lets people know what you do and how you do it better.

d. Keep your business cards in your right pocket. Place their business cards in your left pocket. Be sure to follow up with each person. E-mail has become an extremely popular way of doing that.

e. When you walk in the room, don't look for someone "more important." Chat with the person next to you.

f. Don't give a sales pitch during conversations.

g. Don't overload your follow-up e-mail with information or an attachment. And do not send group e-mails. People like to feel special.

5. Be an individual. It may seem easier to emulate someone else or follow the crowd, but it's not a good idea. You'll lose more and more of yourself, which is difficult to recapture when you finally come to your senses. I realize that our society functions on a "follow the crowd" mentality, but do you really want people to look at you and think that you act just like someone else?

6. Never lose yourself. You're important to this world just the way you are. Don't let negative people or situations change you. Love is about sharing your life with someone. You don't have to lose who you are or surrender your life and dreams to love a person. When you stop being you, your mate has nothing to celebrate. Love is a celebration of uniqueness. When you change to fit someone's mold of who you think they want you to be, you lose the very thing that you and they should love — you. Always seek to grow, learn, and improve, but remember you're okay; the world needs you.

7. Don't try to please everyone. Being a people-pleaser will only make you miserable. Decide what you want to do and bring those who want to come along with you. Don't stress yourself out over the people who will claim that you are stuck up or acting outside of who you are. Be who you want to be. Be who you are.

Think about your life. What will people say about you when you cross over. Complete the following statements.

50. If I cross over today, people would say...

_____

_____

_____

51. When I cross over I would like for them to say...

_____

_____

_____

52. When introducing myself I should say...

_____

_____

_____

53. Every person is within six people of the person I need to meet so I will treat people like...

_____

_____

_____

_____

54. It is important to serve myself before serving others because...

_____

_____

_____

55. The person that is responsible for my life is...

_____

_____

56. My primary goal is to...

_____

_____

_____

57. In order to achieve this goal I need (skills, talents, resources)...

_____

_____

_____

58. The things I need to do today to prepare myself for my future include...

_____

_____

_____

Chapter 7

THE TREASURE IS
IN YOUR HEART

You now have the secret, but the truth to the secret lies within you.

A very dear friend shared this parable with me and I want to share it with you.

An ancient legend tells the story of a group of wise men and women who realized that people did not appreciate the value of happiness and success. They decided to take the secret of happiness and success and hide it where no one would find it. However, they had to decide where they should hide it. A council meeting was called by the chief of the wise men and women to discuss this question. One person said, "Bury the secret of happiness and success in the dark depths of the earth." The chief responded, "No, that will never do, for people will dig deep down into the earth and find it." Another person said, "We should sink the secret of happiness and success into the deep dark depths of the ocean." The chief answered, "No, for the people will dive down into the ocean and find it." A third person said, "We should take it to the top of the highest mountain and hide it there." Again, the chief responded, "No, for the people will climb even the highest mountain to find it and keep it for themselves." The chief gathered everyone around and said, "Here is what we will do with the secret of happiness and success. It will be hidden within every person, because they will not think to look for it there."

This well-done parable brings this book to a close. Some people find the secret to their happiness and success at a young age, some at an old age, and some not at all. Unfortunately, many people travel through life in search of things and people to make them happy. They fail to realize that the secret is held in the depths of their own heart and soul. You now have the secret, but the truth to the secret lies within you. What makes one person feel happy and successful isn't the answer for someone else. For some, it's getting married and having a family. For others it's having a lucrative, rewarding career. And yet for another, it could be traveling around the world enriching the lives of others. There isn't one right answer for happiness and success. The only true answer is the one that your heart and soul responds to.

A wise person listens to and grows from others' experiences, but in order to be truly happy and free you must make and be willing to live with your own decisions. Once you decide what is important to you and what really makes you happy and feel successful, you will be able to make better decisions. Whatever it is that is in your heart to become, you have the talent to make it happen. Don't become frustrated; it takes time to develop your talent. Remember your attitude is going to make the real difference. Be courageous. Stop second-guessing yourself. If you don't try, you already know the result. But when you try, there's no telling what will happen. I guarantee you that you will gain something from the experience.

Each time you challenge yourself to reach a goal, you're developing your gifts and talents. You'll make mistakes, and that's okay. No one has a direct, uninterrupted route to their destiny. As you go within yourself, you'll learn how to embrace challenges. You'll see obstacles as God's way of navigating and guiding you to the right place. With each perceived failure, you'll become stronger and more persistent. The only thing standing between you and your happiness and success is you.

Remember the following key personal essentials to living a power-packed life...

1. Be yourself. Live life on your own terms and according to your own values. Right is right and wrong is wrong. You know the difference. Don't let anyone or anything tell you any different.

2. Make a commitment to something that you enjoy doing. Find something you think you may enjoy and try it. If you decide that you don't enjoy it, that's okay. Don't stop until you experience that undeniable, invisible tug within that motivates you and gives you a thirst to do it over and over again. You'll eventually find your passion, which will lead you to your place in this world. Follow your heart.

3. Don't Give Up! Enjoy the process of living — the ups and downs, the trials and triumphs. Our lives follow a pattern of seasons — learn all you can in each of them. You can successfully live through all of them. When fear tries to stop you, do it anyway. Nothing comes easy. Success requires hard work. Don't obtain a temporary gain that will lead to a permanent loss. Be honest with yourself and others.

4. Have a plan. Ask yourself, "What do I want to achieve?" Write down your vision and then set step-by-step goals that lead to your main goal. When things don't go as expected, be flexible. Always be open to learning. When things get tough, ask yourself: "What do I need to learn from this experience?" Consistently take inventory of your life. Stay in touch with you!

5. Trust yourself and your own opinion of you. Don't let people's opinion of you determine your value. Make sure your decisions reflect that value. It doesn't matter how far you are backed into a corner, you always have options available to you. Choose the best one for you.

6. Embrace change. Change is inevitable. The most successful people adapt quickly and easily.

7. Ask often, "How can I help?" People need you and you need people. Build honest, sincere, dependable relationships. Ask yourself, "How can I help? Why else are we here?"

8. Forgive yourself and others daily. Let your mistakes lead you to greatness. Let other people's mistakes lead you to spiritual freedom. Don't criticize and hold others to a standard of perfection that is impossible to achieve. Forgive, encourage, and love others as yourself.

9. Have your own agenda. Don't let people decide for you what you should be doing. Outline your priorities and make decisions according to those priorities.

10. Never forget that *THERE IS MORE INSIDE*! Always look within for the right answer. Always do your best. Make doing the right thing a priority. In the end, you'll be a better person with a better life. Remember, you won't become what you want; you will become what you believe.

You have the personal essentials needed for living a power-packed life. How do I know the principles in this book work? I know that they work because I live them. And I've helped others to live them. You have to decide if what you are doing right now is working for you. If so, stick with it. If not, make a decision to improve your life. Successful people seek change instead of trying to avoid it. Improving your life doesn't mean you're totally unhappy or discontent with yourself. It simply means "I can and want to be better." As you use the principles in this book, expect improvement. Anticipate your desired results. Give yourself at least thirty days. Let me know how they work for you; I'm anxious to hear from you.

Write me to at:
S. Renee
c/o SRS Productions, Inc.
P.O. Box 177
Dover, DE 19903
or you can visit my website
at www.srenee.com
and follow the link to my email address.

Thank you for inviting me to be a part of your journey. I believe in you. I'm rooting for you. I'm praying for you. You have what you need because *There Is More Inside!*

There Is More Inside is available
at special quantity discounts for
bulk purchases for fund raising, schools,
churches, or any educational use.
For details, visit www.srenee.com
or call (302) 736-5131.

CPSIA information can be obtained at www.ICGtesting.com
Printed in the USA
BVOW08s0215150716

455691BV00001B/31/P